Why We Need the Church to Become More Like Jesus

Why We Need the Church to Become More Like Jesus

Reflections about Community, Spiritual Formation, and the Story of Scripture

Joseph H. Hellerman

CASCADE *Books* • Eugene, Oregon

WHY WE NEED THE CHURCH TO BECOME MORE LIKE JESUS
Reflections about Community, Spiritual Formation, and the Story of Scripture

Copyright © 2017 Joseph H. Hellerman. All rights reserved. Except for brief quotations in critical publications or reviews, no part of this book may be reproduced in any manner without prior written permission from the publisher. Write: Permissions, Wipf and Stock Publishers, 199 W. 8th Ave., Suite 3, Eugene, OR 97401.

Cascade Books
An Imprint of Wipf and Stock Publishers
199 W. 8th Ave., Suite 3
Eugene, OR 97401

www.wipfandstock.com

PAPERBACK ISBN: 978-1-4982-8432-5
HARDCOVER ISBN: 978-1-4982-8434-9
EBOOK ISBN: 978-1-4982-8433-2

Cataloguing-in-Publication data:

Names: Hellerman, Joseph H., author

Title: Why we need the church to become more like Jesus : reflections about community, spiritual formation, and the story of scripture / Joseph H. Hellerman.

Description: Eugene, OR: Cascade Books, 2017 | Includes bibliographical references.

Identifiers: ISBN 978-1-4982-8432-5 (paperback) | ISBN 978-1-4982-8434-9 (hardcover) | ISBN 978-1-4982-8433-2 (ebook).

Subjects: LCSH: Discipleship. Church. Communities—Religious aspects—Christianity.

Classification: BV600.3 H446 2017 (print) | BV600.3 (ebook).

Manufactured in the U.S.A.   11/07/17

Unless otherwise noted, Scripture quotations are from The ESV® Bible (The Holy Bible, English Standard Version®), copyright © 2001 by Crossway, a publishing ministry of Good News Publishers. Used by permission. All rights reserved.

Biblical quotations marked (NASB) come from the New American Standard Bible® (NASB), Copyright © 1960, 1962, 1963, 1968, 1971, 1972, 1973, 1975, 1977, 1995 by The Lockman Foundation. Used by permission. www.Lockman.org/.

Biblical quotations marked (NIV) are taken from the Holy Bible, NEW INTERNATIONAL VERSION®, NIV® Copyright © 1973, 1978, 1984, 2011 by Biblica, Inc.® Used by permission. All rights reserved worldwide.

Dedicated to
my wonderful church family at
Oceanside Christian Fellowship

Contents

Preface | vii

1. Born for Fellowship: Spiritual Formation and the Church as the Body of Christ | 1

2. I Am My Brother's Keeper: Spiritual Formation and the Church as the Family of God | 22

3. When the Group Comes First: Finding a Healthy Faith Family | 40

4. Rooted in the Family of God: Intergenerational Community and Spiritual Formation | 57

5. How We Lost Our Way: The Evangelical Journey from "Us" to "Me" | 79

6. Enjoying the Presence of God: Spiritual Formation and the Quest for Religious Experience | 98

7. Hands to the Plow Together: Community, Mission, and Spiritual Formation | 114

8. Lose the Story, Lose the Community: The Bible, Community, and Spiritual Formation | 127

9. Until Jesus Returns: Eschatology and Spiritual Formation | 144

Conclusion: Why We Need the Church to Become More Like Jesus | 159

Bibliography | 173

Preface

"It is grace, nothing but grace, that we are allowed to live in community with Christian brethren."[1]

— Dietrich Bonhoeffer

RICHARD J. FOSTER PLANTED the seeds for current interest in spiritual formation (SF) when he penned *Celebration of Discipline* back in 1978.[2] The SF movement has since generated countless books and articles and has established itself as a familiar component of theological education in Christian colleges and seminaries across America.

As we might expect, SF has focused primarily on the spiritual development of the individual. Christian community has generally not been at the heart of the discussion.

Proponents have not ignored the church. Virtually every treatment of SF includes some observations about the ways relationships with others contribute to our growth in the Lord. It is fair to say, however, that community has not received the attention in the SF movement that it does, for example, in the Scriptures.

Foster's seminal contribution is representative. Some fifty pages of *Celebration of Discipline* survey what Foster identifies as the corporate disciplines: confession, worship, guidance, and celebration. Well over 120 pages treat individual disciplines such as meditation, prayer, simplicity, and solitude.

Dallas Willard's classic, *The Spirit of the Disciplines*, similarly emphasizes personal practices like "fasting," "frugality," and "sacrifice." Willard gives significantly less attention to the communal aspects of the Christian life.[3]

---

1. Bonhoeffer, *Life Together*, 20.
2. Foster, *Celebration of Discipline*.
3. Willard, *Spirit of the Disciplines*.

Preface

To be fair, neither book was meant to serve as a full-blown treatise on spiritual formation. As the titles indicate, both Foster and Willard focused more narrowly on the spiritual disciplines of the Christian life. The two influential works established a trajectory for SF, however, which would leave its mark on the movement in the decades to follow.

Dietrich Bonhoeffer insightfully cautioned, "Let him who cannot be alone beware of community. Let him who is not in community beware of being alone."[4] SF, particularly in the early years of the movement, addressed its message primarily to the former, that is, to those of us who need to learn how to be alone with God.[5]

The emphasis makes sense in view of our traditional theological taxonomies, which generally distinguish between sanctification and ecclesiology, and which situate the two topics at different places along the theological curriculum. I studied the subjects a year apart from one another, for example, in my MDiv program at Talbot School of Theology back in the 1980s.

Taxonomies function as necessary and helpful ways to organize large amounts of material, and this is certainly the case for the discipline of theology. The threefold message that the above arrangement unfortunately communicates, however, is that (1) sanctification is about my individual development as a Christian, (2) ecclesiology is about the church and its mission, and (3) sanctification is unrelated to ecclesiology. This has made it all too easy to overlook the central role the New Testament assigns to the church in the process of spiritual formation (today's catchphrase for sanctification).

Recent treatments of spiritual life and growth have thankfully become more holistic and interdisciplinary, increasingly acknowledging the role of community in the sanctification process. The edgy title of James C. Wilhoit's book forcefully underscores the need for this course correction: *Spiritual Formation as if the Church Mattered*.[6]

Discussions of the communal nature of sanctification are now commonplace in the literature. Near the beginning of *Foundations of Spiritual Formation*, a textbook for introductory courses in SF, for example, Paul Pettit emphasizes that "*the change or transformation that occurs in the believer's*

---

4. Bonhoeffer, *Life Together*, 78.

5. Thus, Boa considers "Corporate Spirituality" in only the final section (out of twelve) of his widely read textbook, *Conformed to His Image*, 415–49.

6. Wilhoit, *Spiritual Formation as if the Church Mattered*.

Preface

life happens best in the context of authentic, Christian community."[7] Roman Catholic theologian Peter Feldmeier is even more categorical: "There is no such thing as 'Jesus and me.'"[8]

This Book's Contribution

Why We Need the Church to Become More Like Jesus joins what has now become an ongoing conversation about the role of the local church in the spiritual formation of the individual Christian. This book is hardly the last word on the issue. But I hope that the ideas presented in the chapters that follow will open several unexplored avenues for thinking about the relationship between sanctification and ecclesiology.

For better or for worse, my rather eclectic educational and ministerial background has equipped me to float some rather new and, perhaps, scandalous ideas (to American evangelicals) about the importance of community for faith development.

After a rigorous, traditional seminary education in theology and Greek and Hebrew exegesis, I spent the better part of nine years in a doctoral program in the history of Christianity at UCLA, where I was trained in social history and cultural analysis. My dissertation was published in 2001 as *The Ancient Church as Family*.[9] I have been researching and writing about early Christian community and social relations ever since.

I have also been a pastor of a local church for nearly forty years. The combination of real-life ministry experience and academic training has convinced me that we have departed in some profound ways from community as it was understood and practiced in the New Testament church. Until we get a handle on what the early church was actually like—until, that is, our ecclesiology is truly biblical—it seems to me that we are ill-equipped to talk about the role of the church in spiritual formation.

Why We Need the Church to Become More Like Jesus seeks to explore new territory along these lines. We will look at the early church in its ancient Mediterranean cultural setting. Then we will use what we discover about

---

7. Pettit, "Introduction," 19 (italics original). See also Whitney, *Spiritual Disciplines Within the Church*, and, for the practice of spiritual direction, Reed, *Quest for Spiritual Community*.

8. Feldmeier, *Developing Christian*, 29.

9 Hellerman, *Ancient Church as Family*.

Preface

New Testament Christianity to engage in a critique of spirituality and church life as popularly understood among today's evangelicals.

Much of what follows will be culturally and theologically challenging. I encourage you as a reader to approach the material with an open mind, an open heart, and an open Bible.

A final observation is in order before we move into the heart of the book. The approach will be intentionally one-sided. Western evangelicals focus primarily on *me* and God. The book you are about to read deals almost exclusively with *us* and God.

This is not because I think that cultivating a robust personal relationship with God is unimportant. Bonhoeffer is right. Each of us must learn how to be alone with God. I focus on the communal aspect of our faith for two reasons.

First, I feel no need to reiterate what we constantly hear in our churches and read in popular Christian literature. The evangelical community does not need yet another book about how to maximize my personal relationship with Jesus in the context of daily living.

More important is the issue of priorities. As we will discover, the New Testament emphasis is overwhelmingly upon the communal context of spiritual formation, namely, the local church and its mission. To genuinely experience God and grow as individuals, we must get on board with God's program for his people as a whole. God's presence and God's power follow God's priorities.

Many of us long to experience the fullness of God and his purpose for our lives. Not a whole lot of us ever do. The reason, as we will discover, is that we have departed in some significant ways from the biblical view of Christian life and growth.

In recent decades evangelicals have profoundly deemphasized the communal, missional, eschatological aspects of our walk with God in favor of experiencing God in the here-and-now. The time has come forcefully to swing the pendulum back in the biblical direction.

In the final, analysis, the whole argument of *Why We Need the Church to Become More Like Jesus* could be summed up in a single nonnegotiable truth. We grow in our faith as individual Christians to the degree that we are deeply rooted relationally in a local church community that is passionately playing its part in God's grand story of creation, fall, redemption, and restoration.

1

Born for Fellowship

Spiritual Formation and the Church as the Body of Christ

> The pilgrimage of faith must be made in the company of others.
>
> —Sharon Parks[1]

There is good news in the pews. According to a recent Barna study, 77 percent of those who attend church fairly regularly—the study calls them "practicing Christians"—believe it is "very important to see growth in their spiritual lives."[2]

I find it greatly encouraging to discover that so many people in our churches are serious about their relationship with God. The bad news is that more than a third of these well-meaning folks will likely go nowhere spiritually.

Why? Because 37 percent of those practicing Christians claim that they "prefer to pursue spiritual growth on their own" rather than in community with others.

Self-identified Christians who are not involved in a local church are even less inclined to invite others to share their walk with Jesus. A full 41 percent of these consider their spiritual lives to be "entirely private."

The study places the above data under the heading "Discipleship as a Solo Activity?" The question mark at the end of the heading is appropriate.

---

1. Parks, "Love Tenderly," 33.

2. Barna Group, "New Research on the State of Discipleship." The study defines "practicing Christians" as "self-identified Christians who say their faith is very important to their lives and who have attended a worship service, other than for a special occasion, one or more times during the past month."

For discipleship as a solo activity has no place in the biblical picture of spiritual formation.

This chapter and the chapter to follow discuss two key New Testament images of the church: (1) the church as the body of Christ; and (2) the church as the family of God. In each case we will see that we grow in our faith only when we engage in meaningful relationships with others in the local church.

The Individual Christian and the Growth of the Body

Many of us learned to diagram sentences in our seventh-grade English classes. Perhaps you can recall the difference between a main clause and a subordinate clause, an independent clause and a dependent clause.

We still diagram sentences at Talbot School of Theology. Our Greek students learn to diagram sentences in the original language of the New Testament. The discipline of diagramming at times reveals the priorities of a biblical author in ways that are otherwise hard to see.

In Eph 4:15, Paul challenges us to press on to spiritual maturity: "Speaking the truth in love, we are to grow up in every way into him who is the head, into Christ." But just how does that happen? What are the mechanics? What process does Paul have in mind when he thinks of spiritual formation? We find the answer in the next verse:

> *the whole body,* joined and held together by every joint with which it is equipped, when each part is working properly, *makes the body grow* so that it builds itself up in love. (v. 16)[3]

I put the main clause in *italics*. The rest of the verse consists of dependent, subordinate clauses. We can diagram the text as follows:

---

3. I cite the ESV except where noted.

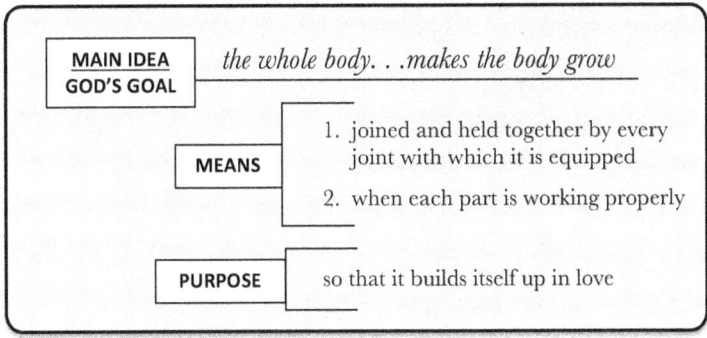

The English diagram accurately reflects the syntax of the Greek original. And it proves to be very revealing.

Note, first, that the main idea—in one of the most important passages about spiritual formation in the New Testament—is not the progress of the individual Christian. Paul's concern is with the growth of "the whole body," that is, with the spiritual health of the community as a whole. The concluding purpose clause confirms this analysis: "so that it" ("the whole body") "builds itself up in love."

God's goal in this Christian adventure is not, first and foremost, my spiritual growth. It is the growth of the community (qualitatively, not quantitatively, in this particular passage).

What about the individual Christian? Paul has not lost sight of your personal pilgrimage. But the way he positions the individual believer vis-à-vis the church body forcefully confronts the me-orientation of modern evangelicalism. The grammar of Eph 4:16 is unequivocal: I as an individual am the *means* to God's overarching *goal* of a healthy, mature church community.

We will want to qualify this, of course. God does not use people in a utilitarian way. But I think you get the point. I am here for the church. The church is not here for me. This much is crystal clear.

The same mindset surfaces earlier in Ephesians, where Paul employs the image of God's people as a temple. Note, again, that the growth terminology is connected with the temple as a whole:

> You are fellow citizens with the saints and members of the household of God, built on the foundation of the apostles and prophets, Christ Jesus himself being the cornerstone, in whom *the whole structure*, being joined together, *grows into a holy temple in the*

Lord. In him you also are being built together into a dwelling place for God by the Spirit. (2:19a–22; cf. 1 Pet 2:4–5)

The metaphor has changed but the corporate focus is the same. In 4:16, "the whole body ... makes the body grow." Here in 2:21, "the whole structure ... grows into a holy temple in the Lord."

We have turned God's priorities upside down. If you are like most American evangelicals, you likely assume that your personal spiritual formation—not the growth of the body—is the goal of the Christian life. And the church is the means to help you become more like Jesus. Our consumer culture has socialized us from birth to attend church primarily to get something out of it: "I am not here for the church. The church is here for me!"

God's priorities are just the opposite. As Paul demonstrates in Eph 4:16, when we connect relationally with others in the community (means #1) and serve one another with our gifts (means #2), God's goal—a relationally healthy, theologically robust body of Christ—becomes a reality in the local church.

Cultivating Christian community and exercising our spiritual gifts are familiar biblical themes, and we will consider each in some detail later in the chapter. We are less familiar with Paul's group-first mentality, however, so we will pause here to unpack this key cultural value before returning to the dynamics of the body metaphor in Ephesians 4.

Paul Was Not Alone

Paul was hardly alone in his preoccupation with the health of God's people as a whole. The apostle's group-first mentality was deeply woven into the tapestry of his Jewish heritage. According to Josephus, a first-century Jewish priest,

> prayers for the welfare of the community must take precedence over those for ourselves; for we are born for fellowship, and he who sets its claims above his private interests is specially acceptable to God. (*Contra Apion* 2.197)

Do not miss Josephus's theological justification for prioritizing "the welfare of the community" over our "private interests": (a) God has designed us this way ("we are born for fellowship"); and (b) it is most pleasing to God ("specially acceptable to God"). In the pages that follow I hope to convince you that Josephus was right on both counts.

Early church fathers held similar views about the relationship between individual believers and the Christian community. Cyprian was the pastor of a large church in Carthage, North Africa, during the middle of the third century. The following citation comes from our earliest surviving commentary on the Lord's Prayer. Cyprian's emphasis on corporate (versus personal) prayer sounds a lot like that of Josephus:

> Before all things, the Teacher of peace and Master of unity did not wish prayer to be offered individually and privately as one would pray only for himself when he prays. We do not say: "My Father, who art in heaven," nor "Give me this day my bread," nor does each one ask that only his debt be forgiven him and that he be led not into temptation and that he be delivered from evil for himself alone. Our prayer is public and common, and when we pray we pray not for one but for the whole people, because we, the whole people, are one. (Cyprian, *The Lord's Prayer*, 8.1)

It is all in the pronouns. Beginning with "Our Father," Cyprian draws our attention to the plural pronouns throughout the prayer that Jesus taught his disciples:

> "*Our* Father in heaven
> hallowed be your name.
> Your kingdom come,
> your will be done,
> on earth as it is in heaven.
> Give *us* this day *our* daily bread,
> and forgive *us our* debts,
> as *we* also have forgiven *our* debtors.
> And lead *us* not into temptation,
> but deliver *us* from evil."
> (Matt 6:9–13)

Pronouns can be revealing. Paul attaches a first-person possessive pronoun—"my" or "our"—to the word "Lord" fifty-four times in his letters. The distribution, however, is anything but even. Paul writes "our Lord" fifty-three times in his letters. "My Lord" occurs only once. Paul's focus, like Cyprian's, is on the community.

The priority that these early Christian leaders assign to the church as a whole grates against our cultural sensibilities. But it made good sense within their social world. Paul and Cyprian were not the only ones who thought that the group should take priority over the individual. Strong-group thinking characterized Greco-Roman society as a whole, and it remains a defining cultural value throughout much of the world today.

Strong-Group Values

For several decades now, leaders in industry have been conducting business across national and cultural boundaries. The American market for Asian products—especially automobiles and electronics—birthed a global economy that has necessitated collaboration among businessmen and -women around the Pacific Rim. In earlier years communication was problematic, however, due to the cultural distance between representatives of American and Asian corporations.

Richard Nisbett sought to address the issue by highlighting the differences between: (a) Asian values, and (b) the contrasting cultural sensibilities of the West.[4] Since the strong-group aspect of Asian culture has much in common with the Greco-Roman world, it will be helpful briefly to summarize Nisbett's contrast between East and West. We begin with several characteristics of our own culture that will be immediately familiar to most readers:[5]

1. Each individual has a set of characteristic, distinctive attributes. Moreover, people want to be distinctive, that is, different from other individuals in important ways.
2. People are largely in control of their own behavior; they feel better when they are in situations in which choice and personal preference determine outcomes.
3. People are oriented toward personal goals of success and achievement; they find that relationships and group memberships sometimes get in the way of attaining these goals.
4. People strive to feel good about themselves; personal successes and assurances that they have positive qualities are important to their sense of well-being.

---

4. Nisbett, *Geography of Thought*, 47–48.
5. Ibid.

Born for Fellowship

This catalog of social virtues fairly describes life as we know it. It would have made little sense, however, to Paul and others in the ancient Mediterranean world.

Let us compare each of the characteristics on Nisbett's list with its strong-group equivalent. If we were to time-travel back to the first century, and spend a good bit of time adjusting to the cultural values and social codes of Paul and his contemporaries, we would find that

1. People are not unique. Groups are unique. A person's tribe or family or village tells you everything you need to know about a person. "Can anything good come out of Nazareth?" (John 1:46). "Cretans are always liars, evil beasts, lazy gluttons" (Titus 1:12). Neither do people want to be distinctive. A contemporary Asian expression aptly reflects the prejudice against individuality that marks all strong-group cultures: "The peg that stands out is pounded down." Thus, when asked to choose from among a group of several yellow pencils and one (unique) green one, 77 percent of the Americans in the study picked the green pencil compared to only 31 percent of the Asian subjects.

2. Individuals do not control their destiny, nor do they see such freedom as particularly desirable. Sons enter into the vocations of their fathers. Young people marry the spouses their parents choose for them, because marriage unites two families, and only those families can determine whether the match is in the interest of the respective kinship groups.

3. Relationships and group membership take priority over personal goals. Goals are not personal to begin with. Success and achievement are measured in terms of how much an individual contributes to the economic viability and public esteem enjoyed by the social group, especially the family. Family honor is everything.

4. Individuals do not attend much to feelings about themselves at all. Psychological introspection as we are familiar with it in the West today was not a pressing concern in Mediterranean antiquity. People prized social status—public honor—rather than self-esteem. A person's primary sense of well-being came from identifying with an honorable social group.

Except for those of Europe and North America, most cultures around the world today remain strong-group cultures. Nisbett's summary of contemporary Asian strong-group values can be adopted as an accurate description of the mindset of individuals in Mediterranean antiquity, as well: "The goal for the self in relation to society is not so much to establish superiority or uniqueness, but *to achieve harmony within a network of supportive social relationships and to play one's part in achieving collective ends*."[6] When we situate the earlier diagram of verse 16 in the broader context of Ephesians 4, we discover that Nisbett's summary corresponds precisely to Paul's understanding of interpersonal dynamics in the body of Christ. We are: (1) to achieve harmony in a network of supportive social relationships ("the unity of the Spirit in the bond of peace" [4:3]); and we are (2) to play our respective parts in achieving collective ends (4:16).

Just a Cultural Phenomenon?

We will return to Ephesians 4 below to consider our roles as individuals in God's community-building project. First, however, we must take a moment to consider the relationship between ancient social values and the timeless truths of Scripture.

We might be tempted to dismiss collectivism as just another cultural phenomenon. Ancient society was strong-group in orientation. Modern America is individualistic. Neither is better. They are simply two different ways of life. In our cultural setting we are not obligated to replicate the collectivist mentality and strong-group solidarity that we encounter among the early Christians. So goes the argument, at any rate.

I want to challenge this kind of thinking from several angles. First, any theology of spiritual formation that purports to be biblical must begin with the nature of God as three persons in perfect communion with one another other, sharing a single divine essence. Scripture firmly grounds the practice of Christian community (the topic of this book), moreover, in the intimacy shared by Father, Son, and Holy Spirit.[7]

We find hints of the connection between God as Trinity, on the one hand, and the social nature of human beings, on the other, as early as the first chapter of Genesis. A Christian reading of v. 26 finds an allusion to

---

6. Ibid., 55 (italics original).

7. Much has been written on the theme. See Morrow, "Introducing Spiritual Formation," 37–41. For more thorough treatments, see Grenz, *Theology for the Community of God*; and Grenz, *Social God and the Relational Self*.

Father, Son, and Holy Spirit in the plural pronouns: "Then God said, 'Let *us* make man in *our* image, after *our* likeness.'"

Could this imply that the image of God in humankind includes a relational component? The verse that follows appears to affirm the idea: "So God created man in his own image, in the image of God he created him; male and female he created them" (Gen 1:27).

When we get to the New Testament, it becomes indisputably clear that (a) our relationships with our fellow Christians are at the very heart of our spiritual lives and that (b) these relationships are grounded in the nature of God himself.[8] Shortly before the crucifixion, Jesus prayed for his followers:

> that they may all be one, just as you, Father, are in me, and I in you, that they also may be in us, so that the world may believe that you have sent me. The glory that you have given me I have given to them, that they may be one *even as we are one*, I in them and you in me, that they may become perfectly one, so that the world may know that you sent me and loved them even as you loved me. (John 17:21–23; italics added)

This is quite astounding. Note the italicized phrase. Jesus prays that his followers will experience the same quality of relationship with one another that he experiences with God the Father.

What cultural orientation to the Christian faith best supports and harmonizes with Jesus's vision? The strong-group church of the early Christians? Or the "just-me-and-Jesus" take on Christianity that marks our lives today? The answer, I think, is obvious.

A second consideration relates to the primary metaphor that the New Testament uses to describe Christian community, namely, the church as a family. Family was the number one locus of relational loyalty in ancient Mediterranean society—the strongest group in a strong-group society.

In chapter 2 we will examine in detail Jesus's view of the church as a family. For the present it will suffice to observe that it would be utterly counterintuitive for Jesus to have chosen family as the primary metaphor for Christian community, if the relational values and practices associated with the metaphor were optional for Christians in other cultural settings. Many of the ethical injunctions (e.g., the "one another"s) in the New Testament, in fact, assume as normative a strong-group, surrogate family setting.[9]

---

8. Davis emphasizes this truth in *Meditation and Communion with God*, 53–54, 67–70.

9. Hellerman, *Ancient Church as Family*; Hellerman, *When the Church Was a Family*.

Why We Need the Church to Become More Like Jesus

It is important to note in this regard that Jesus did not hesitate to overturn those cultural values inimical to the gospel. While he (a) affirmed the collectivist, group-first ideals of his contemporaries when he identified his followers as a surrogate family (Mark 3:31–35), he (b) forcefully challenged the socially stratified honor culture of the Roman world by completely redefining what would be considered honorable behavior in God's family (Mark 10:35–45). This suggests a reasoned intentionality on Jesus's part in both cases.

Finally, the very message of the gospel is an expression of strong-group values—that is, of the notion that the church is not here for me but rather that I am here for the church. It is common for us to say, "Jesus died for my sins." The Bible much more often asserts that Jesus died for *our* sins—the one for the many.

Paul writes in Rom 5:19, for example, "by the one man's obedience the many will be made righteous." According to John's Gospel, the high priest Caiaphas prophesied "that Jesus would die for the nation and . . . to gather into one the children of God who are scattered abroad" (11:51–52). To return to Nisbett's description of strong-group values, above, Jesus played to perfection his respective part as an individual "in achieving collective ends."

It might help to move beyond the pages of Scripture to consider what individualism has done to our broader social environment. Western individualism has had some positive effects on American society. It would be misleading to argue otherwise.

Daniel Yankelovich, however, outlines five negative effects of individualism on American civilization that should give us pause as we consider whether we should pattern our churches after the values of the surrounding culture:

1. decrease in family cohesiveness
2. decrease in feelings of respect for other people and in other moral virtues
3. a sense that everyday life is becoming more impersonal
4. loss of a sense of community
5. loss of a spiritual dimension to life in the wake of the mundane consumerism and materialism of everyday life[10]

---

10. Yankelovich, "Trends in American Cultural Values," 2–9. The five points represent

Every one of these five negative effects flies in the face of Jesus's vision for his followers as reflected in the excerpt from John 17, cited above.

The strong-group approach to community that characterized early Christianity cannot be dismissed as a culturally relative option inappropriate for our churches today. It is grounded in the very nature of our Trinitarian God (John 17:21–23). It was affirmed by Jesus when he identified his disciples as family (Mark 3:31–35). And it was modeled when Christ "gave himself up" for the universal church—the one for the many (Eph 5:25).

A Sanctified Individualism

A word of qualification is in order at this point, as we conclude our discussion of ancient cultural values. Individualism and collectivism are not mutually exclusive options. In any given cultural setting, it will be a matter of emphasis. As we have seen, the biblical worldview clearly privileges the group over the individual.

Yet the Bible does not commend a blind group loyalty devoid of individual identity and autonomy. Overemphasizing group loyalty and solidarity to the exclusion of individual rights and desires creates its own set of problems. There remains a place in a Christian worldview for what we might call a sanctified individualism.

Some passages in Scripture, in fact, explicitly commend culturally subversive behaviors that privilege the individual over the group. Early in the biblical narrative, for example, God commanded Abraham to get up and leave his family. It is hard to imagine a more countercultural expression of individual autonomy than this one, in a strong-group society like the ancient Near East.

How does this square with a collectivist view of Christian community that privileges the welfare of the church over my personal relationship with God? Quite well, as a matter of fact. For God did not call Abraham to a private pilgrimage of spiritual self-actualization. God called Abraham to be the father of the nation of Israel. Abraham exercised his individual choice by choosing to leave one group in order to establish another:

> Now the Lord said to Abram, "Go from your country and your kindred and your father's house to the land that I will show you. And I will make of you a great nation." (Gen 12:1–2)

Johnston's summaries of Yankelovich's findings ("Old Testament Community and Spiritual Formation," 82).

Jesus too challenged his disciples to make costly, countercultural decisions as individuals—decisions that would profoundly affect their lives (Matt 8:21–22; Mark 1:16–20; 10:17–30). In every case, however, the decision was not a choice for *in*dependence. It was a choice for *inter*dependence—a choice for the group. Thus Peter exercised his will as an individual to exchange one family for another:

> Peter began to say to him, "See, we have left everything and followed you." Jesus said, "Truly, I say to you, there is no one who has left house or brothers or sisters or mother or father or children or lands, for my sake and for the gospel, who will not receive a hundredfold now in this time, houses and brothers and sisters and mothers and children and lands." (Mark 10:28–30)

Like us, the early followers of Jesus exercised their wills and made choices as individuals. Unlike us, however, they did not make these choices in the service of personal goals or desires. They chose for the good of the group, the family of God.

We are now prepared to return to Ephesians 4 to explore in more detail how we as individuals fit into God's design for "the growth of the body."

My Role in the Body of Christ

"Joined and Held Together"

The diagram at the beginning of the chapter shows two ways that individual believers contribute to the vitality of a spiritually mature Christian community. The first (means #1) is relational: connecting with others in my church family. Paul uses colorful imagery from physiology to make his point. Due to a slight ambiguity in the Greek, translations of the clause vary. Some assume it is the "joint" or "ligament" that is supplied to the body:

> *joined and held together by every joint with which it is equipped* (ESV)

> *joined and knit together by every ligament with which it is equipped* (NRSV)

It is better to interpret the phrase to mean that the joint or ligament itself does the supplying:

> *being fitted and held together by what every joint supplies* (NASB)
>
> *joined and held together by every supporting ligament* (NIV)

This is confirmed by the parallel in Colossians, where the body is "nourished and knit together through its joints and ligaments" (2:19). Clinton Arnold, in a recent commentary on Ephesians, describes the dynamic reflected in our passage:

> The idea is that the body is comprised of a variety of limbs that are closely connected to one another. Each of these individual members becomes a source of supply for the well-being of all the other members with which it comes into contact.[11]

Don't miss the expressions "closely connected" and "comes into contact." It is clearly the case with the human body that the individual members receive nourishment from the blood only when those members are closely joined to one another by means of the joints and ligaments. If I separate my hand from my arm, the hand will die, and the rest of me will suffer as well.

I learned this the hard way. In the spring of 1994, I took a spill while fishing from a jetty off the Pacific Ocean. I was able to stand back up, but I could not put pressure on my left leg. Something was broken. At the hospital emergency room I found out I had broken my hip. The doctors wanted to rush me right into surgery to set the fracture. They knew something about this particular part of the human body that I learned only later.

The blood supply that runs from the femur to the femoral head (ball of the hip) is very tenuous. If it is compromised at all, the ball of the hip fails to receive its nourishment and necrosis sets in. A full hip replacement becomes the only option. A hip replacement can be a miracle cure for a person in her seventies or eighties. It is not advisable for forty-two-year-old. Yet the severity of my injury was such that a worst-case scenario was a real possibility. Thus the hurry to operate on my hip.

I was fortunate. A brilliant orthopedic surgeon pinned my bones together and the blood supply kicked in several months later. I did not need a hip replacement. More than twenty years later I am still able to jog several miles on the beach with all my original parts.

I learned firsthand that the members of my body must remain "joined and knit together" for each to remain healthy and do its job. The same is true, Paul informs us, in the body of Christ. For the body to grow—and for me to thrive—I need to be relationally connected with others in my church.

11. Arnold, *Ephesians*, 271–72.

"When Each Part Is Working Properly"

It was not enough for that orthopedic surgeon to connect the two parts of my body that had been partially separated by my fall. The blood supply had to kick in as well in order for the physiological magic to do its work. As I mentioned, above, it was not until several months after the surgery that the blood began to flow across the femoral neck. You can imagine how relieved I felt when tests began to show that it had.

To change the analogy, it is not enough to hook up a hose to the water supply. We must turn on the water.

So it is in the church. Relationships among believers (means #1) become effective only "when each part is working properly" (means #2).

"Working properly" could mean any number of things. Given the emphasis on spiritual gifts in the context (vv. 8, 11), however, and the association of the body metaphor with this theme elsewhere in his letters (1 Corinthians 12–14), Paul likely has the exercise of our spiritual gifts in mind. When we serve one another with the gifts God has given us, the Holy Spirit "powerfully works in and through the various members."[12]

Relational intimacy (means #1) and the exercise of our spiritual gifts (means #2)—these two characteristics in the lives of individual church members cause the community as a whole to "grow so that it builds itself up in love" (God's Goal). This is God's design for spiritual transformation, according to Ephesians 4.

The Renewal of the Mind and the Body of Christ

We now turn to Romans 12, where Paul again links the image of the church as Christ's body to the theme of spiritual growth. In contrast to Ephesians 4, however, the Romans passage initially focuses on the dynamics of individual transformation, rather than the health of the community as a whole. The chapter begins with a familiar charge:

> I appeal to you therefore, brothers, by the mercies of God, to present your bodies as a living sacrifice, holy and acceptable to God, which is your spiritual worship. Do not be conformed to this world, but be transformed by the renewal of your mind, that by testing you may discern what is the will of God, what is good and acceptable and perfect. (Rom 12:1–2)

12. Ibid., 271.

Here is one of the most informative passages in all of Scripture about growing in Christ. It is also one of the most potentially misleading if taken out of context.

Read in isolation, Rom 12:1–2 could be understood to imply that the "renewal of the mind" relates solely to the intellectual faculties of the individual believer—that I will be "transformed" only as I saturate my mind with Bible verses and good theology.

This would be to miss Paul's point. To be sure, right thinking is indispensable for progress in the Christian life. But it is never sufficient in and of itself.

The Bible challenges us to love the Lord our God with all of our heart, soul, strength, and mind (Luke 10:27). For many of us, however, the modernist project that began with the Enlightenment has problematized the pursuit of a holistic relationship with God. Modernity encourages us to prize the mind, to value the knowledge of facts over relational intimacy.[13]

In many areas of life this is highly desirable. I would hope, for example, that my accountant would subordinate his knowledge of me as a friend to his cognitive knowledge of the United States Tax Code while he is doing my taxes. And I was delighted that the surgeon who put my hip back together—a total stranger relationally—brought his prodigious knowledge of human anatomy to the operating table that day.

In the spiritual arena, however, things are more holistic. We will consider the significance of the biblical literacy for spiritual formation later in the book. In the present connection it is vital to recognize that an overemphasis on rational appraisal and critical analysis potentially undermines the very relationships we need to thrive in our walk with the Lord.

Knowledge is a volatile commodity. Critical thinking too often breeds a critical spirit. As a pastor and seminary professor, I see the scenario Curt Thompson describes play itself out all too often among believers whose Christianity is overly characterized by a cognitive approach to the faith:

> When you keep your relationship with God exclusively fact-based and rational, it's easy to make judgments about others and yourself. Such judgments reduce your anxiety and increase your sense of safety and protection. However, this way of being also has the

---

13. Mulholland (*Shaped by the Word*, 19–23, 49–63) helps us to see how our "informational-functional culture" has compromised our approach to reading and studying the Bible.

curious effect of increasing the isolation you feel, both from others and within your own mind.[14]

We have all encountered theologically brilliant Christians wholly lacking in wisdom and grace when it comes to interpersonal relationships.

As it turns out, the picture of transformation in Romans 12 involves much more than accumulating a catalog of biblical data. What is in view is a holistic, Christ-centered mindset rooted in Scripture but nurtured and ultimately realized only in community. Thus, in the very next verse, Paul turns our attention to the relational context in which the renewal of the mind occurs, namely, the body of Christ:

> For by the grace given to me I say to everyone among you not to think of himself more highly than he ought to think, but to think with sober judgment, each according to the measure of faith that God has assigned. For as in one body we have many members, and the members do not all have the same function, so we, though many, are one body in Christ, and individually members one of another. (Rom 12:3–5)

Note the connecting conjunction ("For") that begins v. 3. Paul intended for vv. 1–2 and vv. 3–5 to be read together. We cannot experience the change in mindset that Paul talks about Rom 12:2 apart from the body of Christ he describes in vv. 3–5. Transformation happens in community.

Putting Rom 12:1–5 and Eph 4:16 together, we discover that we are "transformed by the renewal of our minds" as we are "joined and held together" in the body of Christ. The "whole body" makes "the body grow"—and we flourish in our individual lives—when we exercise our spiritual gifts in community with one another.

"We Are Born for Fellowship"

The section heading is part of the quote from Josephus cited earlier in the chapter. He believed that God has wired us for community. Recent findings from the field of neuroscience align with the biblical evidence to suggest that Josephus was right.

Paul describes the fruit of the Spirit as "love, joy, peace, patience, kindness, goodness, faithfulness, gentleness, self-control" (Gal 5:22–23). At its most basic level, growing in Christ—spiritual formation—involves

---

14. Thomson, *Anatomy of the Soul*, 23.

growing in these Christian graces. And these attitudes and behaviors are generally learned, practiced, and experienced in the context of interpersonal relationships.

But how do I grow in these attributes? How do I become more patient with my children? More kind to my wife? More responsive to my boss? Experts in the physiology of the human brain offer some fascinating answers to these questions.

In a recent book titled *Anatomy of the Soul,* Curt Thomson delves into the inner workings of the brain to explain an interesting phenomenon that we have all experienced. Imagine you are sitting in a booth at a restaurant with three friends. The waitstaff brings four glasses of water. Five minutes later one of your friends picks up her glass to take a drink. What do you suddenly feel the urge to do? Take a drink of water, of course, whether you are thirsty or not!

Among our various neurological systems is one that researchers have labeled "mirror neurons."[15] The firing of mirror neurons encourages us to mimic the behavior of others. Your system of mirror neurons fired when you saw your friend take a drink of water in the imaginary scenario outlined above.

The same system facilitates the learning of new behaviors. We learn how to use a fork as children, for example, when our mirror neurons are activated and we mimic the activity of an adult across the table. And, interestingly enough, we also learn how to exercise the fruit of the Spirit, at least in part, through the firing of our mirror neurons.

Paul's qualifier "of the Spirit" should not be taken to imply that the character qualities listed in Gal 5:22–23 are uniquely Christian. We have all seen each of these attributes reflected in the lives of unbelievers, often in ways that put many Christians to shame.[16]

Nor is the fruit of the Spirit mysteriously spiritual in the sense that it is unrelated to the physiology of the human body. God has created us as embodied creatures. Unwillingness to embrace this reality is more akin to

---

15. See also Iacoboni, *Mirroring People.*

16. Scholars have found striking parallels in Greco-Roman literature to the catalogs of virtues and vices Paul that includes in his letters (Charles, "Vice and Virtue Lists").

This is not to minimize the role of the Holy Spirit in our lives. However, as one treatment properly notes, "Christian maturity generally correlates with human maturity" (Buckley and Sharp, *Deepening Christian Life,* 4). Steele (*On the Way,* 106) and Feldmeier (*Developing Christian,* 5–13, 232–40) discuss the complex relationship between Christian spirituality and general human maturation.

ancient Gnosticism than to the holistic body-and-soul perspective of the Judeo-Christian tradition.

Thompson uses empathy as an example of a learned behavior that is at the same time an indicator of spiritual maturity. Notice how brain physiology factors into the equation:

> Empathy can be described as an action rather than merely a feeling alone because we demonstrate empathy through nonverbal and verbal clues or actions that project the intent of connecting with another's state of mind. When a child is the subject of another's empathy, he or she will likely undergo the activation of his or her mirror neuron system related to empathy. In other words, *children learn to be empathic with others by seeing it demonstrated toward them.*[17]

For Thompson's empathy we could just as well substitute patience, kindness, faithfulness, or any other fruit of the Spirit. And due to what researchers label the neuroplasticity of the brain, this mimetic learning continues into adulthood.

So, to return to one of the questions raised above: How do I become more kind to my wife? How do I grow in this spiritual character quality?

According to modern neuroscience, one of the ways I learn to be kind is to engage in a close relationship with someone who is kind to me. When I experience kindness expressed towards me, my mirror neuron system is activated and I begin to learn how to "pick up the fork" of kindness, so to speak. Then, as I proceed to exercise kindness in other social contexts, I increasingly reinforce pathways between neurons along this particular neural network, until kindness ultimately becomes a natural part of my life and character.

Add the power of God's Holy Spirit to the mix, and the payoff for spiritual formation should be patently clear. I can go off to my room, read my Bible, and discover that I *should* be kind. But I will likely not *become* kind—and thus grow in Christ—unless I am experiencing mutual kindness in the context of lasting relationships in the body of Christ, "joined and held together by every joint with which it is equipped, when each part is working properly" (Eph 4:16).

Neuroscience likes to say that "there is no such thing as an individual brain, not even an individual neuron."[18] This is not the case physically, of

---

17. Thomson, *Anatomy of the Soul*, 42 (italics added).
18. Ibid., 109.

course. You have your brain, and I have mine. It is true, however, functionally. The neural networks of our brains—which determine our very character—are shaped by interactions with others beginning in infancy and continuing on into adulthood.

The apostle Paul knew quite well what modern neuroscience has only recently confirmed. Character formation occurs in community.[19]

Experiencing God's Love

A final way to appreciate the significance of the body of Christ for spiritual life and growth is to consider the way in which being "joined and held together" in community helps us to experience God's unwavering love for us as individual believers.

Just a few verses before his teaching about "the growth of the body" (4:16), Paul prays for the Christians at Ephesus:

> that according to the riches of [God's] glory he may grant you to be strengthened with power through his Spirit in your inner being, so that Christ may dwell in your hearts through faith—that you, being rooted and grounded in love, may have strength to comprehend with all the saints what is the breadth and length and height and depth, and to know the love of Christ that surpasses knowledge, that you may be filled with all the fullness of God. (Eph 3:16–19)

This soaring prayer is commonly cited as a key piece of evidence that God wants each of us personally to experience his boundless love for us. And so he does!

But how does this occur? How do I grow in my apprehension of God's love? Is it a mystical experience that happens when I pray, or while I am meditating on Scripture? Perhaps. But I rather doubt that this is what Paul has in mind in Ephesians 3.

Consider the literary context surrounding the prayer. Paul's concerns throughout are exclusively communal. The paragraphs leading up to the prayer deal with the status of Jews and Gentiles in salvation history (2:11–22), and with Paul's unique role as apostle to the Gentiles (3:2–15). Immediately following the prayer Paul turns his attention to group dynamics in the church.

---

19. Though it beyond the scope of this project, Paul's imitation language (e.g., 1 Cor 11:1) could be profitably revisited in light of these recent findings from neuroscience as well.

He discusses unity in 4:1–6, and spiritual gifts and the growth of the body in the verses that follow (4:7–16). Personal spiritual formation is nowhere in view in the paragraphs surrounding Paul's prayer in 3:16–19.

When we come to the prayer itself, moreover, we would do well to remind ourselves that Paul prays in 3:16–21 not for individual Christians but rather for a Christian community (the church at Ephesus), with his sights set on the universal church. Thus the doxology that concludes the prayer: "to him be glory *in the church* and in Christ Jesus throughout all generations, forever and ever. Amen" (v. 21).

I do not intend to imply that Paul's prayer does not have in view the apprehension of God's love for us as individuals. The point is that Paul envisions this personal apprehension materializing in a communal setting. He longs for the Ephesians to grasp the depth of Christ's love *"with all the saints"* (3:18). Andrew Lincoln appropriately notes, "The comprehension the writer desires for his readers is not some esoteric knowledge on the part of individual initiates, not some isolated contemplation, but *the shared insight gained from belonging to a community of believers.*"[20]

This brings us back to the notion of relational transformation that has dominated the chapter. How does knowing "the love of Christ that surpasses knowledge" relate to our theme of spiritual formation in the context of community? Or, in Andrew Lincoln's words, how do I gain "insight" into God's love for me "from belonging to a community of believers"?

The answer is simple yet profound. I have become increasingly convinced over the years that we fully experience God's love for us as individuals—and learn how to love him in return—*as we allow ourselves to be known and loved by others in the body of Christ.*

To return, finally, to Eph 4:16, just how far should we press the body metaphor? Further, I suspect, than most of us realize. There is a very real sense in which you and I are the hands, arms, and voice of Jesus in each other's lives. Otherwise, why "the body *of Christ*"? Why not just "the body"?

When the body of Christ is "joined and held together by every joint with which it is equipped," a mysterious dialectic is activated between our relationship with God and our relationships with others. The phenomenon ultimately escapes the analytical efforts of even our brightest theologians. Yet we have all tasted the sweet fruit of this reality.

I experience the compassion of Jesus most deeply when a brother in Christ exercises compassion toward me. God disciplines me most

---

20. Lincoln, *Ephesians*, 213 (italics added).

effectively when that discipline meets me in the form of a loving rebuke from a trusted sister in the Lord. And I will come to understand God's unwavering love for me—to fully experience what it is to be loved by God—when I allow myself to be known by you and discover that you continue to accept me and love me just as I am.

In the words of theologian Mark Saucy, "believers together grow in their own apprehension of God's gracious acceptance as they see it reflected in the deeds of love and forgiveness of their brothers and sisters."[21]

Conclusion

We began by noting that 77 percent of churchgoing Christians in America find it "very important to see growth in their spiritual lives." For those of us who share this conviction, the manner in which Paul connects (a) the theme of spiritual formation with (b) the image of the church as the body of Christ, in Ephesians 4 and Romans 12, underscores a fundamental and nonnegotiable truth about the Christian life: God has designed us to grow in the context of community. Persons like the 37 percent in the Barna Group survey who ignore this reality, choosing instead "to pursue spiritual growth on their own," will experience little or no meaningful progress in their Christian lives.

We turn now to Jesus and the Gospels, to consider the implications of another common New Testament metaphor for Christian community, namely, the church as a family. We will discover that the degree of group loyalty Jesus demanded of his family of followers presents a striking challenge to the popular evangelical view of the local church as a commodity that exists primarily to service the spiritual needs of individual Christians and their natural families.

---

21. Saucy, "*Regnum Spiriti*," 153.

2

I Am My Brother's Keeper

Spiritual Formation and the Church as the Family of God

> The best metaphor for church community is
> the healthy family, not the marketplace.
>
> —Kent Carlson[1]

WE TEACH THROUGH BOOKS of the Bible on Sundays at Oceanside Christian Fellowship (OCF). In the spring of 2009, we were working our way through the Gospel of Mark. I was scheduled to preach on Mother's Day. On holidays we generally depart from our normal routine and deliver a topical message. After thirty years in the ministry, however, I had become more than a little weary of cobbling together Mother's Day sermons.

I received the go-ahead from my fellow pastors to forgo the topical message, continue on in Mark, and recognize the mothers in our congregation during the announcements. On the same day I received the go-ahead, I looked at the schedule to see where we were in Mark's Gospel:

> And [Jesus's] mother and his brothers came, and standing outside they sent to him and called him. And a crowd was sitting around him, and they said to him, "Your mother and your brothers are outside, seeking you." And he answered them, "Who are my mother and my brothers?" And looking about at those who sat around him, he said, "Here are my mother and my brothers! For whoever does the will of God, he is my brother and sister and mother." (Mark 3:31–35)

---

1. Carlson, *Renovation of the Church*, 83.

I Am My Brother's Keeper

Here Jesus tells a crowd of people that his mother is not really his mother. This was going to be a Mother's Day like no other at OCF.

I titled my message "Jesus and His Mommy," and proceeded to inform the congregation that the family of God is more important than our natural families.

Most evangelicals view our relational priorities as follows:

EVANGELICAL RELATIONAL PRIORITIES
#1 = God   #2 = My Family   #3 = God's Family   #4 = Others

That Sunday I tried to convince my people that God's relational org-chart looks more like this:

JESUS'S RELATIONAL PRIORITIES
#1 = God & His Family   #2 = My Family   #3 = Others

The reaction was mixed. Single adults liked the message. Married couples with kids had some reservations.

Casey is a mother and a grandmother. She is one of my favorite people at OCF, in part because I can always count on Casey to speak her mind with the purest of motives. Casey's take on my Mother's Day sermon was this: *Joe, I really liked that sermon. But I don't agree with any of it!*

Casey's reaction to the radical reframing of priorities reflected in the second box above is understandable. I remain convinced, however, that Jesus's relational priorities make the most sense of our Lord's troubling teachings about family in passages like Mark 3:31–35.

Gaining clarity here is vital for our spiritual lives. Chapter 1 maintained that spiritual formation occurs primarily in the context of community. The Bible uses the family metaphor more often than any other image to describe Christian community.

The family idea is much more common, for example, than the metaphor of the body of Christ that we examined above. Think how often you encounter the word "brother" when you read your New Testament. How many times is God called "Father"? Now add in related terms from the semantic field of kinship, such as "children," "adoption," "heirs," and "inheritance." The family metaphor shows up everywhere.

If I desire to grow in Christ, it only follows that I will want to understand what it means for me as an individual to be a part of the family of God. This brings us face-to-face with the radical redirection of family loyalties reflected in Jesus's teachings in the Gospels.

Jesus and Family—A Mixed Bag

To accurately assess what Jesus had to say about family we must come to grips with three kinds of family teachings in the Gospels. During my message that Sunday, I titled the categories as follows: (1) Happy Family Passages, (2) Not-So-Happy Family Passages, and (3) Surrogate Family Passages. Categories 1 and 2 have to do with the natural family. Category 3 describes the church family. Here are some examples of each category:

#1—Happy Family Passages

> Matt 15:3-4—"And why do you break the commandment of God for the sake of your tradition? For God commanded, 'Honor your father and mother' and 'Whoever reviles father or mother must surely die.'"

> Matt 19:3-6—And Pharisees came up to him and tested him by asking, "Is it lawful to divorce one's wife for any cause?" He answered, "Have you not read that he who created them from the beginning made them male and female, and said, 'Therefore a man shall leave his father and his mother and hold fast to his wife, and the two shall become one flesh'? So they are no longer two but one flesh. What therefore God has joined together, let not man separate."

#2—Not-So-Happy Family Passages

> Matt 10:21—"Brother will deliver brother over to death, and the father his child, and children will rise against parents and have them put to death."

> Matt 10:34-36—"Do not think that I have come to bring peace to the earth. I have not come to bring peace, but a sword. For I have

come to set a man against his father, and a daughter against her mother, and a daughter-in-law against her mother-in-law. And a person's enemies will be those of his own household."

Matt 8:21-22—Another of the disciples said to him, "Lord, let me first go and bury my father." And Jesus said to him, "Follow me, and leave the dead to bury their own dead."

Luke 14:26—"If anyone comes to me and does not hate his own father and mother and wife and children and brothers and sisters, yes, and even his own life, he cannot be my disciple."

#3—Surrogate Family Passages

(Some of these also fit under #2.)

Mark 3:31-35—And his mother and his brothers came, and standing outside they sent to him and called him. And a crowd was sitting around him, and they said to him, "Your mother and your brothers are outside, seeking you." And he answered them, "Who are my mother and my brothers?" And looking about at those who sat around him, he said, "Here are my mother and my brothers! For whoever does the will of God, he is my brother and sister and mother."

Matt 5:23-24—"So if you are offering your gift at the altar and there remember that your brother has something against you, leave your gift there before the altar and go. First be reconciled to your brother, and then come and offer your gift."

Matt 18:15—"If your brother sins against you, go and tell him his fault, between you and him alone. If he listens to you, you have gained your brother."

Matt 18:35—"So also my heavenly Father will do to every one of you, if you do not forgive your brother from your heart."

Mark 10:28-30—Peter began to say to him, "See, we have left everything and followed you." Jesus said, "Truly, I say to you, there is no one who has left house or brothers or sisters or mother or father or children or lands, for my sake and for the gospel, who will not receive a hundredfold now in this time, houses and brothers and sisters and mothers and children and lands, with persecutions, and in the age to come eternal life."

The list is not exhaustive. Other passages could be placed in each category. But this representative sampling plainly reveals the challenges we face in trying to harmonize what Jesus said about family into a coherent set of values and priorities.

It will not do to ignore or downplay one set of passages in favor of another. A holistic treatment of family in the Gospels must find room for all three kinds of family sayings. This is not the place, however, to handle these texts in detail. I have done that elsewhere.[2] We will grapple with the topic of Jesus and family in more general terms.

First, notice how few Happy Family Passages are listed above. Several years ago I was invited to contribute a chapter to a Christian education textbook on family ministry. The author's expertise was in education, not biblical studies, but he wanted to build his theology of family ministry on a solid scriptural foundation. He asked if I would write a chapter on Jesus and family in the Gospels.

What my colleague had in mind, of course, was a chapter about Jesus and the natural family. I politely declined the invitation, telling him that I did not think that there was enough material to write a theology of family from the Gospels. Honor your parents. Stay married. There may be more, but not much more.

Many more passages in the Gospels represent categories 2 and 3 above than category 1. This is also true of Paul's letters, where church family language abounds ("brother," "Father," "inheritance," "adoption," "children of God") and texts about natural family relations, as informative as they are, are few and far between (1 Cor 7; Eph 5:22–6:4; Col 3:18–20).

Two Key Issues: Theological Dissonance and Family Loyalty

The three categories of family sayings in the Gospels raise two significant issues that can help us to harmonize them.

Issue #1: Theological Dissonance

The first issue is obvious: the jarring dissonance that obtains between the happy family passages, on the one hand, and the not-so-happy family passages, on the other.

---

2. Hellerman, *Ancient Church as Family*; Hellerman, *Jesus and the People Of God*; Hellerman, *When the Church Was a Family*.

I Am My Brother's Keeper

Consider the matter of our attitude toward our parents. In one place Jesus says, "Honor your father and mother" (Matt 15:4). Elsewhere, in the same Gospel, he tells a man who wants to bury his father, "Leave the dead to bury their own dead" (Matt 8:22). Neither Jesus nor Matthew seems to have a problem with these two apparently contradictory sayings coming from the mouth of the same individual. And then there is Luke 14:23: "If anyone comes to me and does not hate his own father and mother. . .he cannot be my disciple." Dissonance indeed!

Issue #2: Family Loyalty

The second issue raised by the Gospel evidence is not self-evident to modern Western readers, but it would have been immediately apparent—and highly troubling—to Jesus's earliest followers. What I have in mind is the loyalty conflict unavoidably and forcefully raised by the very idea of belonging to two families, a natural family and a faith family.[3]

As we have seen, the ancient world was strong-group culture where loyalty to the group took precedence over individual goals and desires. The most important group in the ancient world was the family. This meant that loyalty to family constituted the paramount relational virtue for persons in the New Testament world.

To help us understand what family loyalty would have signified in Jesus's day, I have substituted the word *family* where the author used the word *group* in this informative description of strong-group values from the pen of Bruce Malina:

> The person perceives himself or herself to be a member of a [family] and responsible to the [family] for his or her actions, destiny, career, development, and life in general. Correspondingly he/she perceives other persons primarily in terms of the [families] to which they belong. The individual person is embedded in the [family] and is free to do what he or she feels right and necessary only if in accord with [family] norms and only if the action is in the [family's] best interest. The [family] has priority over the individual member, and it may use objects in the environment, other groups of people in the society, and the members of the [family] itself to facilitate [family] oriented goals and objectives.[4]

---

3. Christians from strong-group cultures continue to wrestle with this issue. See, for, example, Yep et al, *Following Jesus*.

4. Malina, *Christian Origins and Cultural Anthropology,* 19.

The subordination of individual desires to the interests of the family as a whole is most obviously reflected in the practice of arranged marriages. In the ancient world parents chose mates for their children, because only the parents—who were networked in the broader village community—could determine whether a particular match between two individuals was in the interest of the family unit. And this is the key point. In the New Testament world, it was all about the interests of the family as a whole.

In such a cultural environment it becomes easy to see how Jesus's challenge to join a new family would raise serious questions among his followers about the vexing issue of family loyalty. *To which family do I now owe this strong-group allegiance, this undying relational loyalty?*

As we have seen, American evangelicals typically do an end run around the problem by separating loyalty to God (#1) from loyalty to God's family (#3), and then placing loyalty to natural family (#2) in between:

EVANGELICAL RELATIONAL PRIORITIES
#1 = God   #2 = My Family   #3 = God's Family   #4 = Others

This, however, will not work, because I cannot be a follower of Jesus without being a loyal member of his group.

This is a crucial consideration. During his earthly ministry Jesus did not call individuals into a private relationship with him. He challenged them to join a movement. He called them to become part of a new family. And it was within this new family—and only within this family—that Jesus' followers related to him one-to-one. As Paul would put it several decades later, using a different metaphor, "we were all baptized into one body" (1 Cor 12:13).

The notion that loyalty to God could somehow be separated from loyalty to God's family is a fabrication of popular Western evangelicalism that was nowhere on the radar screen of Jesus and the early Christians. In the words of Cyprian of Carthage (c. 250 CE), "He who does not have the church for his mother cannot have God for his Father" (*On the Unity of the Church*, 6).

An analogy may help. I jog on the beach for exercise. My hometown (Hermosa Beach, California) is quite affluent, so I often run past people who can afford to pay others to guide them through their daily workouts. The sociology of these training sessions varies. Some folks hire a personal

I Am My Brother's Keeper

trainer who "disciples" them one-on-one in their exercise program. Others (presumably with less discretionary income) belong to groups of people led by a trainer of some sort. A Pilates class I often see while jogging is an example of the latter arrangement.

The point here is that the dynamics of the Christian life are more like that experienced by a student in a Pilates class than a fellow with his personal trainer. The Pilates student relates to her instructor as part of a group. We relate to Jesus as part of his family.

Every analogy ultimately breaks down. My relationship with Jesus is much more personal than a relationship with one's Pilates instructor. (You will not find a Pilates instructor who "knows what you need before you ask" [Matt 6:8].) And it is also the case that my relationship with my fellow Christians is (or ought to be) a whole lot closer than interpersonal relationships among those who attend a twice-a-week exercise class. Analogies only go so far.

But I trust you get the point. Western evangelicals tend to think of Jesus as a "personal spiritual trainer" with whom we interact alone, apart from relationships with our brothers and sisters in Christ. This allows us to distinguish between loyalty to God and loyalty to God's family. This is decidedly not how the early Christians conceived of their relationship with God and his church.

We can further illustrate this by way of historical analogy. It comes as a bit of a surprise to many Christians to learn that Jesus was not the only one who claimed to be the messiah or a divinely inspired prophet in first-century Palestine. Josephus narrates the rise and fall of several such figures. We read about some of them in the New Testament. Consider the words of Gamaliel before the Sanhedrin:

> "Before these days Theudas rose up, claiming to be somebody, and a number of men, about four hundred, joined him. He was killed, and all who followed him were dispersed and came to nothing. After him Judas the Galilean rose up in the days of the census and drew away some of the people after him. He too perished, and all who followed him were scattered." (Acts 5:36–37)

Elsewhere in Acts we read of an "Egyptian . . . who recently stirred up a revolt and led the four thousand men of the Assassins out into the wilderness" (21:38).

Jesus, of course, was the only messianic claimant whose messiahship was authenticated by his resurrection from the dead. He was the real thing.

Why We Need the Church to Become More Like Jesus

In an important sociological sense, however, the Jesus movement directly paralleled the other renewal movements mentioned above. Notice in the above citations that each of these movements involved a group of people. Members did not relate to their leaders solely as individuals. In every instance—including the Jesus movement—loyalty to a leader was tangibly expressed by loyalty to his group and its mission.

Loyalty to Jesus's group, however, meant becoming part of a new family. Here Jesus appears unique, since we do not read of Theudas, Judas the Galilean, or the Egyptian framing their movements in terms of surrogate family. Jesus drew upon kinship terminology again and again to describe relations among his followers, and the result was a direct and profound challenge to natural family loyalty for anyone who wanted to develop an ongoing relationship with Jesus.

Putting It All Together

We now return to our two sets of relational priorities:

EVANGELICAL RELATIONAL PRIORITIES
#1 = God   **#2** = My Family   **#3** = God's Family   **#4** = Others

JESUS'S RELATIONAL PRIORITIES
#1 = God & His Family   **#2** = My Family   **#3** = Others

Which set of relational priorities best addresses the two key issues—theological dissonance and the challenge of family loyalty—raised by our three kinds of family teachings in the Gospels?

Evangelical relational priorities privilege the natural family (#2) over the faith family (#3). This certainly solves the vexing problem of family loyalty. It does so in favor of the natural family. So far, so good.

How about the issue of theological dissonance? If anything, evangelical relational priorities exacerbate the problem. For the more we prioritize natural family relations in the teachings of Jesus, the less sense we can make of the not-so-happy-family passages. *Why would a profamily Jesus say so many harsh things about the family?* I find the dissonance generated by this approach to be intolerable.

How do Jesus's relational priorities fare? Here God and his family (#1) take priority over our natural families (#2). The problem of conflicting family loyalty is again solved, but this time in favor of the church family.

This is a hard set of priorities for modern evangelicals to embrace. But notice that the theological dissonance raised by the not-so-happy passages now finds adequate explanation. Jesus lived in a strong-group culture where family loyalty reigned supreme. If, as Jesus's relational priorities assume, Jesus intended to establish a new faith family (one that would take priority over the natural family), he would obviously have needed to challenge natural family loyalty again and again during his earthly ministry. This is precisely what we find in the Gospels.

Important Qualifications

Did I do a better job convincing you than I did convincing Casey with that Mother's Day sermon? If you remain troubled, some crucial qualifications may help clarify what God has in store for us here.

Qualification 1: The church is a family, not a business.
It is an organism, not an organization.

When I preached from Mark 3:31–35 that Mother's Day, I purposely did not use the word "church" until the end of the message, when I introduced this series of qualifications. Most Christians do not know what "church" means, in the biblical sense of the word, and my challenge to prioritize church above family would have been completely misunderstood if I had continually referred to Jesus's alternative family as "church" throughout the message.

The word translated "church" in our Bibles simply means a "gathering" or "assembly" of people. For the early Christians, church was not a place. And it was certainly not an institution with a building, a budget, and a myriad of efficiently run programs. Unfortunately, the very fact that we can (a) talk about going to church, or (b) ask, "How was church, today?" shows that when we think of church, the first thing that comes to mind is (a) a place to go with (b) programs to evaluate.

Qualification 2: The commitment to which Jesus calls us is a relational commitment, not an institutional commitment.

This qualification follows naturally from the previous one. We will need to learn to think of church in relational terms before we will ever be willing to make the kind of commitment to Jesus's family that characterized the early Christians. The chief biblical metaphors for the people of God—the body of Christ and the family of God—are deeply relational in nature, as we have seen. To become a follower of Jesus is to become loyal to the *people* of God, not to a pastor's vision or to the demands of a large church's calendar of programs.

I am well aware that churches need structure and organization to facilitate people-oriented ministry. Without a degree of institutional efficiency, I would not receive a paycheck for my part-time job at OCF. And my sermon notes would not show up in the Sunday bulletin.

But it remains the case that ministry is about people. And the commitment we make when we join a local church is a commitment to our brothers and sisters in the family of God.

Qualification 3: Jesus's relational priorities are not to be used as an excuse to sacrifice my family on the altar of Christian ministry.

The danger of confusing a relational commitment with an institutional commitment is very real. The church planter who started OCF in 1986 (I joined the staff in 1996) was a close friend with whom I had ministered at a previous church. Our families vacationed together and our children played together. In 2000, while we were serving as the two full-time co-pastors, Chris's wife and four teenagers informed him that they wanted nothing more to do with Chris, his church, or his God. A divorce followed, the family left the church, and Chris left the ministry to teach in the public schools. It is not God's intention for Jesus's relational priorities to be used as an excuse for a pastor to be away from his family, involved in church programming and counseling night after night each week.

I Am My Brother's Keeper

Qualification 4: Believers in my natural family remain my first relational priority among the people of God.

Paul wrote, "If anyone does not provide for his relatives, and especially for members of his household, he has denied the faith and is worse than an unbeliever" (1 Tim 5:8). I tell my young adult daughters, Rebekah and Rachel, "You are my daughters for a season, my sisters forever." On this side of eternity, while Rebekah and Rachel remain my daughters, they (and their mother) are my most important surrogate siblings at OCF.

This may sound like a return to our evangelical relational priorities. It is not. Rather, in this scenario I am situating my natural family as my first relational priority under the overarching rubric of the family of God. This is markedly different from viewing the two groups as distinct social entities that compete with one another for time and resources, and then prioritizing my natural family over my church family.

This scenario helps me to think of my natural family as being organically embedded in the family of God. The word "embedded" comes from Malina's description of a strong-group family, referred to earlier in the chapter. Since this idea is better "caught than taught," we will unpack the concept with a series of illustrations of what it means to be embedded in the family of God in chapter 4.

A dilemma surfaces, of course, when a member of my natural family is not a member of my faith family. At this point a loyalty crisis inevitably emerges, and there is no one-size-fits-all solution. Such situations are best addressed on a case-by-case basis. I trust you can see, however, that Paul's concern that believers not become "unequally yoked with unbelievers" (2 Cor 6:14) takes on a new sense of urgency when we begin to conceive of church—and loyalty to our church family—as the early Christians did.

Crucial Observations

How does all this ecclesiology cash out in real life, where I have to juggle between allegiance to God's family and my commitment to my natural family? Two observations pretty much sum it up.

Observation #1: The family of God is not here to serve my family. My family is here to serve the family of God.

This should look familiar. We encountered the idea that I am here for the church—the church is not here for me—in our examination of Eph 4:15–16, in chapter 1. What applies to me as an individual member of the body of Christ also applies to my family as a whole. My family is here for the church. The church is not here for my family.

Consumerism in the culture at large has all but hijacked this biblical mindset. Christian parents now view church as just another resource to help them raise well-rounded, self-motivated kids, who will be able effectively to navigate life when they reach adulthood. Sunday school on Sunday, AWANA on Wednesday, soccer on Tuesday, ballet on Friday, music lessons on Saturday—the list of experiences that affluent American parents seem to think their kids need in order to become successful, productive adults, goes on and on.

Families taken captive by this deceptive cultural mandate have no time left to develop the kind of close relationships with other believers that the early Christians enjoyed. Without such relationships, spiritual formation comes to a virtual standstill for parents and children alike.

Brandon Cash, one of my co-pastors at OCF, is a wise father of four kids ranging in age from seven through seventeen years old. Brandon allows each child to choose to participate in only one non-school or non-church activity at a time. Brandon and his wife, Courtney, want to make sure that Abigail, Esther, Sarah, and Judah have plenty of time each week to hang out with their church family, often in informal settings, in order to develop meaningful relationships with people of all ages at OCF. The Cashes know very well that (as we saw in chapter 1) Christian character development occurs in close association with others who love Jesus—not by participating in a myriad of time-consuming extracurricular activities.

Playing sports or participating in a community theater production are great ways to develop qualities like teamwork and self-discipline. Cultivating close relationship with our brothers and sisters in the family of God is the only way to become more like Jesus. Both are necessary. But Brandon and Courtney properly recognize that the latter is more important than the former. It is a delight to see their four kids actively involved in various aspects of ministry at OCF and enjoying every minute of it. The Cash kids are truly growing in the grace and knowledge of their Lord Jesus Christ.

Observation #2: More than a family that is not, a family that is deeply embedded in the broader family of God will be (a) healthier spiritually as a family group and (b) more effective for the kingdom of God.

What is true of us as individuals is also true of our natural families. We are made to thrive in the community of God's family. The Cashes, mentioned above, are a good example of a natural family that is deeply embedded in the family of God at OCF.

Again, it is easier to recognize what "embedded in the broader family of God" means than to define it. In chapter 4 you will encounter several first-person stories that will help illustrate the concepts we are wrestling with here.

Single Adults, Same-Sex Attraction, and the Family of God

Because of the potential conflict of family loyalty involved with Jesus's relational priorities, we have spent a lot of time talking about family. We must now expand the second observation above, to include not just those who are married with kids, but everyone who is a follower of Jesus: *More than a Christian who is not, a Christian who is deeply embedded in the broader family of God will be (a) more spiritually healthy and (b) more effective for the kingdom of God.*

According to the most recent (2010) U.S. census, 43.6 percent of the U.S. adult population are unmarried. Our theology of family in most evangelical churches is so biblically out of balance, however, that we are left with virtually nothing of substance in the way of a theology of singleness and celibacy.

Much of this is understandable. Marriage and family have been under siege in America ever since the sexual revolution of the 1960s. The Christian church responded by placing its focus squarely on the family in recent decades.

The result of all this, however, for the increasing numbers of singles (of whatever sexual orientation) in society and in our churches has not been positive. By giving disproportionate attention in sermons and in church programming to marriage, parenting, and family dynamics, we essentially communicate to unchurched single adults that there is no place for them among God's people.

Those courageous unmarried believers who do struggle to find a place in our churches encounter a different but equally disheartening message. I served as a pastor to single adults for five years. I interacted with enough unmarried adults to appreciate how they view the church and, more important, how singles think the church views them. The message we unwittingly communicate to our unmarried brothers and sisters runs something like this: *You will only grow up and become a real adult Christian when you get married and have a family.*

Sermons and books that extol the marriage relationship as the primary place wherein spiritual growth occurs unfortunately reinforce this message. In retrospect, I think that the same thing happens when churches (with the best of intentions) hire a pastor of single adults and program life-stage ministries targeted at unmarried folks in the congregation.

We can trace the theological roots of this unbiblical view of singleness and marriage to evangelical relational priorities that privilege the natural family over God's family and thereby encourage an overly family-centered ministry. The biblical priorities we encounter in Jesus's relational priorities encourage us to focus instead on the church family, which includes, of course, persons of every marital status.

When we allow the family of God to occupy first place in our hierarchy of relational loyalties, marriage ceases to be *the* crucible for spiritual formation and becomes one of any number of church family relationships that provide a context for growth in Christ. Now even a single adult like the apostle Paul can begin to make some progress in a walk with the Lord!

The New Testament commends the body of Christ—not marriage—as the community in which spiritual growth occurs (Eph 4:15–16). I am not implying that God does not use our relationships with our spouses to grow us up in Christ. I am simply suggesting that God can and does work the same miracles of transformation in relationships with other members of our church family.

To come at this in another way, consider Jesus's final charge to his disciples in the Gospel of Matthew, the Great Commission:

> "All authority in heaven and on earth has been given to me. Therefore go and get married and make babies in every nation, teaching them to be responsible, productive citizens who grow up, get married, and make babies of their own. And surely, I am with you always, even when you become grandparents."

I Am My Brother's Keeper

That, of course, is not the Great Commission. But you might not know it by our church programming, much of which seems to be based instead on the charge to "be fruitful and multiply" in Gen 1:28, a command that is nowhere reiterated in the New Testament.

The Great Commission is about a different kind of procreation entirely:

> "All authority in heaven and on earth has been given to me. Go therefore and make disciples of all nations, baptizing them in the name of the Father and of the Son and of the Holy Spirit, teaching them to observe all that I have commanded you. And behold, I am with you always, to the end of the age." (Matt 28:18–20)

Among the early Christians, marriage and singleness were both subordinated to an overarching passion to obey the Great Commission and win the world for Christ.

The two themes of ministry and marital status intersect most clearly in 1 Corinthians 7, where Paul views marriage as "a concession" to our physical desires (v. 6) and commends singleness as the superior way to be "devoted to the Lord in both body and spirit" (v. 34, NIV). In 1 Corinthians 7, Paul responds to a potentially problematic assumption of the Corinthians: "It is good for a man not to marry" (v. 1). In course of the ensuing discussion we learn much about Paul's convictions concerning singleness:

> I wish that all men were as I myself am. (v. 7)
>
> To the unmarried and the widows I say that it is good for them to remain single as I am. (v. 8)
>
> I would like you to be free from concern. An unmarried man is concerned about the Lord's affairs—how he can please the Lord. But a married man is concerned about the affairs of this world—how he can please his wife—and his interests are divided. An unmarried woman or virgin is concerned about the Lord's affairs: Her aim is to be devoted to the Lord in both body and spirit. But a married woman is concerned about the affairs of this world—how she can please her husband. I am saying this for your own good, not to restrict you, but that you may live in a right way in undivided devotion to the Lord. (vv. 32–35, NIV)
>
> So then he who marries his betrothed does well, and he who refrains from marriage will do even better. (v. 38)

This is not all Paul says about marriage, of course, but it is pretty much all he says about singleness (cf. 1 Cor 9:5). And it is the only place in the Bible where singleness and marriage are evaluated side by side for their respective abilities to facilitate "the Lord's affairs" (v. 34).

We may give lip service to 1 Corinthians 7, but the way we do church proves to be the litmus test for our theology of marriage and singleness. What follows is an excerpt from a story that ran on the front page of the print edition of the *New York Times* on March 22, 2011:

> Like all too many Americans, Mark Almile, age 37, was laid off in the spring of 2009 when his workplace downsized. He has been searching for an appropriate position ever since, replying to more than 500 job postings without success.
>
> But Mr. Almile, despite a sterling education and years of experience, has faced an obstacle that does not exist in most professions: He is a single pastor, in a field where those doing the hiring overwhelmingly prefer married people and, especially, married men with children.
>
> "I'll get an e-mail saying 'wonderful résumé,'" Mr. Almile said in an interview. "Once I say I'm single, never married, I never hear back." Mr. Almile has been shocked, he says, at what he calls unfair discrimination, based mainly on irrational fears: that a single pastor cannot counsel a mostly married flock, that he might sow turmoil by flirting with a church member, or that he might be gay.[5]

Apparently, someone has not read 1 Corinthians 7.

Or Acts 21. In Acts 21:9, we encounter Philip's "four unmarried daughters, who prophesied," presumably in the context of house-church meetings in Caesarea Maritima. Here we have (1) young (2) single (3) women exercising what Paul identifies as the most desirable spiritual gift in the early church (1 Cor 14:1). Any one of these three characteristics would disqualify Philip's daughters from engaging in their prophetic ministry in more than a few of our churches today.

The fact remains that most adults will ultimately marry. But many will not. And those who do are marrying later in life, often leaving a decade or more of single adulthood between adolescence and matrimony.

And then there are those Christians among us who experience same-sex attraction, and who may need to commit to lifelong celibacy to live in a manner pleasing to the Lord.

---

5. The article appeared online a day earlier: Eckholm, "Unmarried Pastor."

I find the Bible to be unequivocally clear in limiting sexual intimacy to the relational context of heterosexual marriage. Same-sex marriage is not an option for a professing Christian. To proclaim this truth with any prophetic credibility, however, the evangelical church will need to provide familial support and companionship for our gay and lesbian brothers and sisters who determine to remain celibate in order to be faithful to Jesus.

The spiritual formation of our unmarried brothers and sisters—of whatever sexual orientation—depends upon a biblical theology that (1) situates both singleness and marriage under the overarching rubric of the family of God, (2) encourages singles and families in the church to cultivate meaningful relationships across the generations, and (3) mobilizes all to use their gifts to further the cause of the gospel in a way that fits their current life situation.

Conclusion

We have now considered two principal images used to describe the church in the Bible. Chapter 1 introduced the idea of strong-group community and emphasized the relational intimacy involved in the New Testament picture of the church as the body of Christ (Romans 12; Ephesians 4). Chapter 2 focused on the metaphor of the church as a family and Jesus's radical challenge to rethink our family loyalties (Mark 3:31–35). In both cases, we have encountered a view of Christian community that differs significantly from popular conceptions of church in America today.

Some of you will be immediately drawn to the idea of a strong-group church family. Others will struggle with the idea, perhaps because you had a bad experience in an unhealthy community in the past.

The kind of commitment to the body of Christ (chapter 1) and the family of God (chapter 2) described above is not optional, however, if we wish to grow in our walk with the Lord. A deeply relational, strong-group ecclesiology is biblical. God has designed us for it.

The potential for abuse in a strong-group setting, however, remains very real. If I am going to prioritize the good of the community over my personal walk with Jesus, I will need to exercise some of the "sanctified individualism" discussed in chapter 1 to make sure that I wisely choose the right church family. The next chapter outlines several characteristics of healthy Christian community.

3

When the Group Comes First

Finding a Healthy Faith Family

> The character of the community shapes the character of its people.
> —Craig Dykstra[1]

Let us revisit a revealing portion of Bruce Malina's portrayal of the strong-group mindset and substitute "church family" where appropriate: "The individual person is embedded in the [church family] and is free to do what he or she feels right and necessary only if in accord with [church family] norms and only if the action is in the [church family's] best interest."[2] A description such as this offends our modern sensibilities. With the qualifications outlined in the previous chapter firmly in place, however, the above citation paints a reasonably accurate picture of the way the early Christians viewed their relationship to the local church.

What does it mean for me to be "embedded in my church family and free to do what I feel is right and necessary only if in accord with church family norms and only if the action is in the church family's best interest"? *What if my church is an unhealthy community that inhibits rather than encourages the spiritual formation of its members?*

This is a crucial consideration for anyone longing for the kind of church family relationships enjoyed by the early Christians. The potential for personal growth in the context of such relationships is great. But so is the potential for abuse.

As a church leader I must do all I can to ensure a healthy, nurturing social environment for those in my trust. And as an individual Christian I

---

1. Dykstra, *Vision and Character*, 55.
2. Malina, *Christian Origins and Cultural Anthropology*, 19.

must develop the discernment necessary to distinguish between a healthy and an unhealthy community.

Transformational Communities

Psychologists have come to recognize that spiritual transformation "will always unfold within and between communities of others who either facilitate or impede awakening and unfolding."[3] The notion of community embeddedness, originally a social anthropological concept, now appears in the psychological literature as well. Robert Kegan, for examples, prefers to talk about people as "embedduals" rather than as individuals, and underscores the power of community to influence our attitudes toward life: "At this very moment your own buoyancy or lack of it, your own sense of wholeness or lack of it, is in large part a function of how your own current embeddedness culture is holding you."[4] An important recent treatment of Christian spiritual formation, by respected psychologist and spiritual guide David Benner devotes a whole chapter to "The Communal Context of Transformation."[5]

Therapists are particularly sensitive to the negative potential of community to inhibit growth, perhaps because of time spent with persons who have been emotionally and spiritually traumatized in hurtful group settings. Benner offers a prescription for healthy community that he feels will facilitate, rather than impede, the spiritual unfolding of its members: "Environments that support growth, transformation, and human becoming must do three things: They must hold, they must then let go, and they must stick around long enough so that we can be reintegrated in the next community that will hold us."[6] The second and third tasks are crucial because "Life is a succession of holding environments and cultures of embeddedness." "To hold without constraining is the first requirement of care."[7] Benner is adamant about this: "No single thing could make a bigger positive change in the growth and development of persons than an increase in the number of communities that understand the first rule of care to be holding without constraining and that learn to celebrate when

---

3. Benner, *Spirituality and the Awakening Self*. I will interact with Benner through much of the chapter.
4. Kegan, *Evolving Self*, 116.
5. Benner, *Spirituality and the Awakening Self*, 173–89.
6. Ibid., 185.
7. Ibid., 176.

Why We Need the Church to Become More Like Jesus

members are ready to move beyond the community."[8] Benner proceeds to relate a positive and a negative example of "holding without constraining," each involving a young person needing to expand horizons beyond the boundaries of a fundamentalist Christian upbringing.

In one case the family encouraged and facilitated that growth. Their daughter, Erin, transitioned in a healthy way from one holding community (the family's legalistic church) to the next (a campus ministry with "a broader faith tradition").

Bas had the opposite experience. He too began his spiritual life in a fundamentalist religious environment. Bas's pilgrimage was gravely compromised, however, by an authoritarian father who felt threatened by Bas's need to transcend the boundaries of his Dutch neo-Calvinist upbringing. Ultimately, Bas was disowned by his father and theologically chastised by his family's pastor when he shared with his family his excitement about a spiritual awakening he had experienced in another church in the area.

Healthy and unhealthy ways of community holding profoundly affect the future trajectory of their members' spiritual lives. Erin integrated her earlier experience into her later life and, as a result, she continues to grow in her faith. Unhealthy holding results instead "in a disruption of development that leaves many people stuck for the rest of their lives in postures of dis-identification (being against beliefs and practices that previously defined them)."[9] By his late twenties, Bas had become an atheist. Twenty years later, "his creativity had dried up" and "his soul had atrophied."[10]

I commend Benner for his efforts to be fair. In neither scenario is Christian fundamentalism portrayed as intrinsically problematic. The deciding factor is the manner in which the respective communities did or did not facilitate the transitions of their young people to their new community settings.

As Benner elaborates upon the kind of community that best nurtures the spiritual formation of its members, however, a distinct bias emerges. A genuinely transformational community "welcomes diversity in terms of ethnicity, sexual orientation, economic and social status, political beliefs, and so forth."[11] "Conservative," it turns out, is a dirty word for Benner:

8. Ibid., 185.
9. Ibid., 179.
10. Ibid., 184.
11. Ibid., 185.

> When "conservative" is used as an adjective to qualify anything, part of what it is describing is a desire to conserve. In churches, the focus of that conservative instinct is usually theology, and so tight boundaries are placed around theological understandings that are considered to be orthodox, and everything outside this is marked as heretical or liberal. This means that what you think and how you approach certain questions are either within this boundary or outside it. Consequently it is not surprising that the community constrains members to stay within this boundary, or why someone who moves outside this boundary is viewed as a threat.[12]

Conservative Christianity is a problem after all. The contrasting example of a healthy transformational community, which Benner proceeds to relate in the same paragraph, confirms this. The mission statement of a church that "seems very successful in allowing people the freedom to be able to grow and change" reads as follows:

> As a community we welcome and celebrate human diversity—including spirituality, ethnicity, gender, and sexual orientation. We aim to create a space where people of any faith or none can question and discover the sacred in life through openness, struggle, and prayer, and in common commitment to be in solidarity with the poor and marginalized, and to cherish Creation.[13]

Striking a Balance

Benner's convictions about community and spiritual formation resonate warmly with postmodern values of ideological relativism and social inclusivity. His ideal transformational community contrasts sharply, however, with church as we encounter it in the New Testament and in early Christianity. This is understandable, since Benner's view of spirituality owes more to what has come to be known as Perennial Philosophy—"timeless truths that lie at the basis of [all] the world's wisdom traditions"—than to the more circumscribed teachings of the New Testament.[14]

I find it hard to imagine, for example, that Paul would have encouraged and facilitated the transition of a believer who felt the need to leave the church in Corinth in order to move on to her next culture of embeddedness.

---

12. Ibid., 187.
13. Ibid. Benner cites the church's "service bulletin."
14. Ibid., 20.

Indeed, the very idea of an individual transitioning from community to community, which is at the heart of Benner's thesis, would have been an anomaly in the world of the New Testament.

The cultural contrast surfaces when Benner draws upon family dynamics to substantiate his view: "Good parents prepare their children for independence, and good communities should do the same."[15]

Only in the modern West. Independence, in this sense, was not a virtue in the ancient world. Maturity was.

In antiquity, parents did not raise their children to become independent of their communities of origin. They socialized them to become healthy adult members of those communities. Public rites of passage in all traditional societies, such as today's Jewish Bar/Bat-Mitzvah or the assumption of the *toga virilis* ("toga of manhood") in ancient Rome, serve(d) precisely this function.

Psychological differentiation is the fruit of good parenting in every culture. Sociological independence—required by Benner's conviction that spiritual transformation involves "a succession of holding environments and cultures of embeddedness"—is a parenting goal unique to the modern West.

Benner would likely respond by maintaining that the modern worldview is superior in this regard. In an early chapter of *Spirituality and the Awakening Self*, he describes three evolutionary stages in the development of human consciousness:

1. a magical, egocentric worldview (c. 300,000–8000 BCE)
2. a mythical, ethnocentric worldview (c. 8000 BCE–1500 CE)
3. a modern, world-centric worldview (c. 1500 CE–the present)

These stages in the evolution of human consciousness parallel three stages of spiritual enlightenment, so that "Every one of us can move from egocentric to mythocentric (or ethnocentric) and then to world-centric frames of reference for relating to that which is beyond us. Every one of us can experience a broadening of our perspectives on life that offer our spirits more freedom to soar."[16] Notice what has happened here. The modern, world-centric view of the West has conveniently become the desired goal of both human society as a whole and individual spiritual transformation. This

15. Ibid., 176.
16. Ibid., 31.

strikes me as just another sophisticated way of normalizing our modern Western worldview as the defining metanarrative against which to evaluate other cultural constructs.

For more than two millennia Christians have drawn upon a different metanarrative to decide what community and spiritual transformation should look like: the story of the people of God in the Bible, which reached its climax in the ministry of Jesus of Nazareth and the outpouring of the Spirit at Pentecost.

We will explore the community-defining function of stories in a later chapter. Suffice it to say that every community has a story that tells its members who they are vis-à-vis the world around them, and which thereby reinforces their sense of social solidarity. And in each case, the defining story serves to articulate and strengthen community boundaries.

Paul did, in fact, encourage someone to leave the Corinthian church. He challenged the community to excommunicate a man who refused to embrace the community's shared beliefs and behaviors (1 Cor 5:1–13). Paul clearly did not share Benner's aversion to "tight boundaries" that "are placed around theological understandings that are considered to be orthodox." His communities utilized the very boundaries that trouble Benner in order to determine who was in and who was out, theologically and behaviorally.

The degree of diversity that Benner advocates for a healthy transformational community turns out to be a postmodern ideal that ultimately has no corollary in real life. The very idea of community assumes a set of values and convictions that outsiders do not share. As social scientists will be quick to inform us, a community with no boundaries is no community at all.

There is also a strain of consumerism in Benner's approach to community, which privileges the individual over the group and that views communities as resources whose sole raison d'être is to facilitate the process of personal transformation: "communities exist for the support of others."[17]

Taken as a whole, Benner's approach to spiritual transformation will resonate more with Unitarian Universalists than with orthodox Christians of any stripe. And yet Benner is right in so many ways:

1. Communities often seriously compromise the spiritual progress of their members when they are threatened by those who challenge their boundaries and traditions. A healthy community allows room for its

---

17. Ibid., 178.

members to question and dialogue about the community's beliefs and practices.
2. Individuals generally make healthy transitions from adolescence to adulthood in their spiritual lives when those transitions are encouraged and facilitated by mentors in the community.
3. Communities that most effectively engender spiritual growth in their members are communities that are themselves open to transformation.

Can we benefit from these insights and still maintain a biblical view of Christian community as a strong-group surrogate family whose defining scriptural narrative establishes robust theological and behavioral boundaries? I believe we can. And I believe we must.

Marks of a Healthy Christian Community

The negative potential of dysfunctional communities to obstruct spiritual formation underscores the need to develop the discernment necessary to distinguish between healthy and unhealthy churches. It is time to consider what a healthy Christian community might look like.

We mapped out the biblical contours of community in chapters 1 and 2, with the metaphors of the body of Christ and the family of God, respectively. Here we will complement the biblical materials with the insights Benner provides. What follows is not an exhaustive list of characteristics (biblical or otherwise) of a local church. Practices such as the teaching of the Word, and the sacraments of baptism and the Lord's Supper, are assumed. Our focus here is on the relational health of the community, particularly as a context for the spiritual transformation of its members.

1. A Healthy Church Will Be Theologically Centered

My conversion to Christ in 1975 initiated a journey that has been at once both spiritual and intellectual. I have earned five graduate degrees, written seven books, and taught in a graduate school of theology for more than two decades. The uninformed might think that Dr. Joe Hellerman knows just about everything there is to know about the Bible and the Christian life.

Nothing could be further from the truth. Here is how I describe my intellectual pilgrimage to date: *I have become more and more certain about fewer and fewer things.*

Does this mean that someday I will be absolutely certain about nothing? Of course not. Rather, my confidence in the central tenets of orthodox Christianity has become stronger and stronger over the years, while my convictions concerning peripheral issues have become more and more tentative. A church that desires to provide room for the transformation of its people will take a similar approach to the doctrines and practices of the faith.

The point of contention, of course, will be the dividing line between that which is central and that which is peripheral. Different churches will draw the line in different places.

I would want my church, for example, to view as theologically non-negotiable such doctrines as the inspiration of the Bible, the deity of Christ, penal substitutionary atonement, the historicity of the resurrection, and the future return of Jesus. I would have serious reservations, however, about joining a church that defined itself by its views on the so-called charismatic gifts, the doctrine of election, the chronology of end-time events, the role of church in society, or Christian consumption of alcohol—to name but a few issues that I find peripheral. Your list of essentials and nonessentials will likely differ.

This is not to say that a church should not hold and teach positions on nonessentials. It is simply to say that those positions should not be taught in such a way as to imply that persons in the congregation who think differently are somehow less spiritual. Indeed, it is hard to imagine how a church could function without some consensus among its leaders, for example, about the appropriate context for the exercise of charismatic gifts. But a healthy community will welcome dialogue about such issues and—if nonessentials are truly nonessential—will be open to change should God lead the church in a new direction.

2. A Healthy Church Will Be Sensitive to Process

We return now to Benner's threefold model—(1) holding, (2) letting go, and (3) staying to facilitate transformation—but with an important caveat. I agree with Benner that a healthy community should serve its members in these three capacities. I am not convinced, however, that our faith transitions inevitably necessitate leaving one community to join another.

Benner notes that he was "quite taken back by the arrogance" displayed by a group of church leaders who thought that their church could provide what their people needed "for every stage of their spiritual journey."[18] If these pastors were thinking institutionally, about a series of life-stage ministries in their church, for example, perhaps Benner's reaction was justified. But assuming that the provision in view has to do primarily with a community's *people*—not its programs—I find the general intentions of these leaders to be quite biblical.

As we saw in chapters 1 and 2, transformation occurs in the context of intimate surrogate family relationships. Such relationships often take years to develop. It strikes me as counterproductive for a Christian to sever these relationships, in order to join a new community that appears to be a better fit for his or her evolving spiritual needs.

There will always be exceptions, as illustrated by the examples of Erin and Bas, above. But a healthy church will generally have all the resources necessary to facilitate the spiritual transformation of its members within the context of that community itself.

For this to occur, however, the church needs to be highly sensitive to the variegated spiritual growth processes of its individual members. Community leaders in particular must learn how wisely to hold, let go, and support transformative change in the lives of those under their care. This assumes a markedly relational—rather than institutional—mindset, as we discussed in chapters 1 and 2. Leaders will know their people, and their people will know—and be known by—one another.

I spent my most formative years as a Christian in just such a community. I was a pot-smoking rock musician when I began my spiritual quest in the fall of 1974. When I became a follower of Jesus a year later, I somehow landed in a very conservative Conservative Baptist church. Except for a bit of institutional calcification in some quarters among the old guard, however, Community Baptist Church was remarkably healthy. I was received with open arms.

Shortly after I arrived, I became involved in a young adult group with several older adult mentors who deeply understood spiritual formation, long before the moniker ever surfaced in the literature. These leaders wisely allowed me the space and the time I needed for a postconversion pilgrimage that was messy both morally and theologically.

I had been involved in the young adult group for a year or so. Phyllis, our Bible teacher, knew that I was sleeping with a young lady in the group.

---

18. Ibid., 177.

Phyllis also knew that the Holy Spirit was giving me grief about it, so she left me alone for some time to let God to do most of the work.

One day, as part of a general conversation about my future vocational plans, Phyllis almost casually remarked, "Joe, you need to get out of that relationship." I was caught off guard in the best sort of way. I knew Phyllis cared for me and had my best interests in view. An arrow pierced my heart and the immoral relationship soon ended.

I was a bit of a theological maverick as well. Before I converted to Christianity, I had spent the better part of a year dabbling in Eastern mysticism. After my conversion I remained pluralistic in my theology. I knew Jesus was the answer for me. I was not convinced that he was the answer for everyone.

Today the ideological exclusivity of Christianity is one of my nonnegotiables, a theological "hill to die on." But it took me several years to become sufficiently impressed by the absolute uniqueness of Jesus to embrace this central tenet of Christian orthodoxy. Phyllis and other church leaders were content to patiently wait, while I continued to grapple with this issue and with other community beliefs and behaviors that I struggled with early on.

Notice that the uniqueness of Jesus is not a peripheral doctrine. Newcomers to the faith sometimes need a good deal of time and space to fully embrace their community's defining beliefs and behavioral standards. Dialogue should be encouraged and questions welcomed.

I will always recall my watershed moment along these lines. What I am about to relate was not a defining moment for me theologically, though theology was certainly involved. It was a defining moment for me relationally. The experience left me with a textbook example of what a healthy community—embodied in the sensitivity of its leaders—can do to facilitate significant transformation in the life of a church member.

I had been at Community Baptist for two years and had volunteered in various capacities. After I had directed a youth choir for several months, Duke, the youth pastor, asked me to serve in the high school department. I was assigned the freshmen boys.

Working with those kids proved to be more meaningful than anything I had ever done. Little did I know that I was taking my first intoxicating steps along a lifelong trajectory that God had mapped out for me as a minister of the gospel.

I did not know that, but apparently our youth pastor did. Just a few months later, in June 1978, Duke asked me to take over a high school group of some sixty young people so he could find time to finish seminary. I would be responsible for teaching the group on Sundays and for overseeing all their events and activities.

I responded by throwing up a theological smokescreen that would have surely derailed the process in a more institutional, theologically protective, church setting. "Hey, Duke," I replied, "what if I don't believe in Noah's ark or some of those other stories in the Bible?"

Duke replied, "Joe, you don't know what you believe yet. We'll keep you on a short leash and make sure you get some formal theological training. What do you say? You know those kids really love you."

How could I say anything but yes? To my surprise, Duke convinced the senior pastor and the deacon board to hire me half-time for four hundred dollars a month on the condition that I begin classes at the local seminary. I was off and running in vocational Christian ministry, and I have never looked back.

In the two decades that followed, Community Baptist Church paid my way through seminary, hired me as their full-time pastor of single adults, and financed my PhD at UCLA. I met my wife, Joann, at the church and both of our kids were born while I was on staff. Our family thrived for years in the relational soil of this wonderful Christian community.

Now what if Community Baptist Church had been an institutionally driven church that made decisions "by the book" rather than in response to the unique, often messy, spiritual needs of the community's individual members? Phyllis could have found plenty of Bible verses about sexual immorality to warrant kicking me out of that young adult group. The theological smokescreen I tried out on Duke would surely have raised grave concerns among the church's ideological gatekeepers about Joe Hellerman's Christian orthodoxy.

My first two years as a follower of Jesus had hardly generated the kind of spiritual resumé that qualified me to be high school director at Community Baptist Church. I still marvel at the fact that the church took a chance on me. Somehow, in the delightful mystery of God's providential care, I began my Christian journey rooted in a healthy church family, where I was deeply known by others who had mastered the art of "holding without constraining."[19] For that I remain forever grateful.

19. Ibid., 185.

3. A Healthy Church Will Be Open to Change

In a helpful treatment of Christian formation, Lee Steele rightly rejects any view that posits a final and identifiable destination along the path to Christian maturation. On this side of eternity we never "arrive." We are always in process. Embracing this reality is itself an evidence of growth: "Maturity can be understood as openness to growth."[20]

What is true of individual believers in this regard is also true of Christian communities. A church that is open to change sends a powerful message to its members that encourages them to welcome transformation in their personal lives, as well. Few communities, however, are genuinely open to change, and the inevitable alternative is calcification.

Institutional calcification is a universal phenomenon. Those who study the life-cycles of churches trace four common stages: (1) a *man* with a vision initiates (2) a *movement,* which becomes (3) a *machine* that ultimately calcifies into (4) a *monument.*[21] At stages 2 and 3 members often thrive and grow. A community that has settled into stage 4 provides little room for the spiritual transformation of its constituency. Churches that are intentionally open to change have the potential to avoid this progression, but institutional calcification is a formidable and persistent adversary.

To strike a balance between openness to change and the preservation of a meaningful community culture is to engage in a delicate dance. Most of us stumble to the side of overprotection, generally resisting change. This is certainly my tendency, at any rate.

I like my church just as it is. And I want to keep it that way.

Some of our newcomers think otherwise. They arrive at OCF with agendas determined by previous church experiences. They want us to change our values and ministries to align with their own ecclesiastical convictions.

Unchurched folks who come to Christ at OCF are a different story entirely. Our church is their first Christian community experience. Their

---

20. Steele, *On the Way,* 85. Virtually all contemporary treatments of the Christian life view spiritual formation as a process the *telos* of which will only be reached "when we see him" and become fully "like him" (1 John 3:2; cf. Nelson's title, *Spiritual Formation: Ever Forming, Never Formed*).

21. This particular formulation is attributed to by some to Richard Rohr (Ohmer, "Man, Movement, Machine, Monument"). Others trace it to Vance Havner (Demore, "Man, Movement, Machine, Monument").

appreciation and gratitude for the way we run our services and our programs is at times almost palpable.

These patterns have influenced my attitude toward change in the church. I find myself wanting to protect OCF from perceived corruption at the hands of church-hoppers whose convictions about congregational life are different than mine.

Margy Emmons, our worship leader, has helped to expand my horizons along these lines. Margy rightly reminds our pastoral team that God brings new people—even some from other churches—to OCF for a reason. God desires to make OCF into something better through the passions and convictions that these newcomers bring to the party. Most of them, at any rate.

Of all people I ought to recognize this. Did I not emphasize in the previous chapter that the church is first and foremost an organism, and not an organization? Organisms are living entities that change and grow. To inhibit that growth is to guarantee institutional calcification and ultimately death.

Within the boundaries of orthodox theology and praxis, then, a healthy church will be a community that changes and grows in response to its constituency and to the ever-changing contours of its surrounding community. Members will assimilate this posture of openness and become open to transformation in their own lives, as well.

4. A Healthy Church Will Be Led by Pastors in Community

If genuine transformation occurs "only within a communal and interpersonal context," to quote Benner, then it only makes sense to think that church leaders should be in community as well, both to experience and to model what it means to be changed by others.[22]

A leader in relationship with no one is in a precarious place spiritually. He or she also subtly but powerfully communicates to church members that they do not need close relationships to grow in their spiritual lives either. "As go the leaders, so goes the church."[23]

---

22. Benner, *Spirituality and the Awakening Self*, xii.

23. Scazzero, *The Emotionally Healthy Church*, 36. Hendricks undertook a study of men who failed in ministry for moral reasons. He writes:

> When I asked them to tell me about their accountability groups, every one of the participants except one responded, "I have no accountability group and never had

When the Group Comes First

The Bible makes a strong case for pastors being in two kinds of relationships: (1) with other leaders in the church, and (2) with a representative handful of the people they serve. I have written extensively on these ideas, so I will limit my comments here. In *Embracing Shared Ministry*, I maintained that a local church should be led by "a plurality of pastor-elders who relate to one another first as siblings in Christ, and who function only secondarily—and only within the parameters of that primary relational context—as vision-casting, decision-making leaders for the broader church family."[24]

Eight pastor-elders share the responsibility for shepherding the people of OCF. We meet each Tuesday morning to share our lives and to pray for one another. We do little or no church business at these weekly gatherings. Rather, we deal with the nuts-and-bolts of ministry and programming—what most people regard as church leadership—when we come together again, in a different context, on the first Saturday of every month.

Five of us have been part of the team for nearly two decades. The others have come on board in the years since. As you might imagine, the relationships we have cultivated at those Tuesday meetings now run very deep. They are genuinely life-giving.

The above arrangement simply reflects (at the top level of church leadership) our conviction that the family of God is, first and foremost, a living, relational organism, and only secondarily an institution that requires vision casting, strategic planning, and administrative oversight. The result, in our case, has been a remarkably healthy team of leaders who send a vital message to our people: spiritual formation occurs in community for every follower of Jesus—even the church's shepherds.

The notion that pastors should be relationally connected to the people they serve (#2, above) is potentially more challenging, especially as our churches get larger and larger.

---

one" ("Forward," 13).

In this regard, I find it highly revealing that the chapter titled "Leadership and Spiritual Formation," by Seidel (177–94) contains not a word about leading in community with others. This otherwise excellent contribution would be more accurately titled "The Leader's Identity in Christ."

24. Hellerman, *Embracing Shared Ministry*, 17. More and more churches are successfully experimenting with plurality leadership. Note, for example, Lueken's pilgrimage as the co-pastor of Oak Hills Church in Northern California (*Renovation of the Church*, 88–97).

Why We Need the Church to Become More Like Jesus

Many of us assume that people who attend a megachurch do not experience authentic Christian community. That is what I thought as well until I was properly chastised by a group of students I taught in an adult degree completion program at our Biola extension site in Laguna Niguel, California. Much to my surprise, I discovered that these students were enjoying a profound community experience in their small groups at the "mega of all megas," Saddleback Church.

As it turns out, large churches that care about such things—and Saddleback obviously does—typically have the resources to get a greater percentage of their people into community than is the case in smaller congregations with fewer staff members and less administrative support. People in those megachurches participate in Christian community with their fellow church members in some very meaningful ways.

Community among church members, however, is not the only kind of community necessary for support and progress in the spiritual life. The New Testament also emphasizes community between leaders and followers, between shepherds and sheep, between those who teach the Word and those who hear their teaching. Here, I suggest, is where some of our larger churches inevitably run off the tracks of New Testament ecclesiology.

Consider Paul's ministry among the Thessalonians:

> Being affectionately desirous of you, we were ready to share with you not only the gospel of God but also our own selves, because you had become very dear to us. (1 Thess 2:8)

Paul communicated the truth at Thessalonica in a deeply relational context.

We encounter the same dynamic in Paul's farewell address to the Ephesian elders (Acts 20). Paul claims that he "did not shrink" from declaring to the Ephesians "the whole counsel of God" (v. 27). Notice, however, that we do not find Paul in Ephesus (a) teaching God's Word in an impersonal auditorium filled with several thousand people who cannot possibly have access to him relationally or—perhaps worse yet—(b) functioning as a talking head on a screen imparting the Word at a remote video venue. Paul taught the Bible in relationship with those who were on the receiving end of his instruction.

In Acts 20, the theme of relational ministry forms a powerful literary *inclusio* (a sandwich effect, of sorts) that marks the beginning and the end of the passage. Paul begins his address by reminding the Ephesians, "You yourselves know how I lived among you" (v. 18). Then, at the end of the passage, the response of Paul's converts confirms the relational nature of his ministry among them:

> And there was much weeping on the part of all; they embraced Paul and kissed him, being sorrowful most of all because of the word he had spoken, that they would not see his face again. (vv. 37–38)

The point here is straightforward. The New Testament model of ministry finds the teacher of the Word in close relationship with—and directly accessible to—those who are taught the Word. How else could Paul challenge his converts to imitate his life priorities? (1 Cor 4:16; 11:10; Phil 3:17; 1 Thess 3:7, 9)

Perhaps one could argue that the kind of relational ministry reflected in the New Testament is descriptive of early church practice and not normative for us today. Perhaps it is perfectly acceptable for me to be fed the Word by a stranger from a distance on Sundays, while a midweek small group leader or extension campus pastor shepherds me in my daily walk with God.

Perhaps. But when (a) the whole law is summed up in the command to "love your neighbor as yourself" (Gal 5:14), and when (b) we are to be known as Christians by the quality of our relationships (John 13:35)—in summary, *when healthy relationships are at the very heart of all we are and do as Christians*—can we really dispense with something so central to New Testament church life as the relational connection between the teacher and the hearer of the Word? I think not.

During my first year of seminary, a seasoned pastor some thirty years my senior warned me never to develop close relationships with individuals in my congregation. For all of the above reasons, I tell my seminary students just the opposite: do not take a job in a church *unless* the leaders—particularly the senior leader—*are* in relationship with others in the church family.

Ideally this should be true not only of our pastor-teachers but also of those who lead us in worship. Last Sunday, at OCF, a young woman named Kelly Olson sang "Your Love Never Fails." I sat in the front row looking up at Kelly and found myself particularly touched by her solo during the song. When I later reflected on my experience, the reason I was so moved by Kelly's performance became perfectly clear.

For one thing, Kelly nailed the song. But musical skill during worship, while necessary (I would have been hopelessly distracted if she had sung out of tune), is never sufficient. What pierced my heart was not that

Kelly nailed the song. It was that *Kelly* nailed the song. What made the song meaningful was the nature of my relationship with the person who was ministering to me on our worship team.

I have known Kelly for the better part of eighteen years, since she was in grammar school. She is the daughter of one of my fellow pastors. Dan and his wife have two daughters the same age as mine, so the four girls have grown up together as part of our OCF church family. I had the privilege of seeing God set Kelly's heart on fire for him as a young adult, and I've watched her grow in the Lord ever since.

So when Kelly Olson sings, I listen in a way that I would never listen to a stranger or paid professional brought in to sing a Sunday solo with OCF's worship team.

Conclusion

God has wired us for deep and lasting relationships with our brothers and sisters in Christ. He has created us to thrive and grow in the context of such relationships. This explains why many of us long for the kind of community experienced among the first followers of Jesus.

Attaching myself to a strong-group community that functions like the early church, however, is risky business. I might be utterly transformed. Or I might be deeply wounded. The spiritual and relational health of my community of embeddedness will most often be the determining factor.

We considered four marks of a healthy church family:

1. *A Healthy Church Will Be Theologically Centered*
2. *A Healthy Church Will Be Sensitive to Process*
3. *A Healthy Church Will Be Open to Change*
4. *A Healthy Church Will Be Led by Pastors in Community*

In our broken world there are no guarantees we will not be poorly served—even deeply wounded—in the healthiest of churches. The four characteristics outlined above will go a long way, however, to provide nourishing relational soil for us to "grow in the grace and knowledge of our Lord Jesus Christ" (2 Pet 3:18).

4

Rooted in the Family of God

Intergenerational Community and Spiritual Formation

> We have been saved for community.
>
> —John Jefferson Davis[1]

WE HAVE ALL HEARD it said that some ideas are "better caught than taught." I have certainly found this to be the case with the notion of strong-group community, which has been the topic of the first three chapters of this book. We turn now to several stories about how the church has functioned as a family in the lives of some of the folks at OCF where I serve on a team of pastor-elders.

Two of the narratives illustrate how formal programming can be leveraged to fan the fires of relational intimacy in our churches. The third story reveals the power of an informal, grassroots approach to community-building.

Two of the stories are first-person accounts from individuals in our congregation. In the remaining narrative a father (the author) describes his oldest daughter's remarkable pilgrimage, as she discovered her calling in the arts as part of her OCF church family.

Making Difficult Decisions: Oceanside Christian Fellowship's Wisdom Councils

One of OCF's most meaningful ministries is something we call the wisdom council. A wisdom council is an ad hoc gathering for persons

---

1. Davis, *Meditation and Communion with God*, 88.

desiring input from others for major life decisions not addressed by the moral absolutes of Scripture.

A church member initiates a request for a council. The couple that heads up the ministry then recruits a pastor and six or seven other persons with life experience related to the decision in question. Because council topics are extremely varied, there is a different mix of people around the table at every wisdom council. Here are just a few of the issues addressed in recent years:

- *Is this a wise direction to grow and expand my business?*
- *Should I evict a problem renter? If so, how?*
- *How should I respond to these divorce papers?*
- *Should I change careers?*
- *I've been unfairly let go from my job. How should I proceed?*
- *What role should I play in the life of a homeless man?*

What all these decisions have in common is the need for wise counsel from persons who are not directly involved in the situation at hand.

One of our earliest requests for a wisdom council came from a young mother named Marina Wallis. Marina will tell her story:

> Several years ago our church announced a new ministry called a wisdom council. As I listened to the pastor explain it, I imagined what a sacred haven it could be for someone facing a difficult decision in his or her life. Little did I know that this "someone" would be me just five months later.
>
> It was August 2012. I had just taken a year off from a decade of volunteer service for Young Life, a ministry that reaches out to unchurched youth. My extensive responsibilities had included overseeing the ministry's budget, growing and recruiting leaders, organizing fundraising events, and doing a whole lot of other behind-the-scenes work.
>
> I had poured myself into Young Life, which made it difficult to step down, because I knew all too well that the harvest was ripe, while our laborers were few. However, my husband and I had decided to homeschool our children. I needed time to figure out the world of homeschooling and all the responsibilities it entailed.
>
> Now, after a wonderful year of working with our oldest child, homeschooling had become quite manageable. But I could never seem to get those Young Life teenagers off my mind. I began to wonder, *could I*

Rooted in the Family of God

step back into leadership while continuing my role as stay-at-home mom and homeschool teacher?

Young Life needed leadership. And I knew God had given me talents that could fill the need. My heart's desire was to be faithful to Jesus' command to "Go and make disciples." Jesus didn't say "Go, if it's comfortable," or "Go, if it's convenient," or "Go, if you're single," or "Go, if you're without kids."

But the idea of operating in an effective, healthy way at home and in the ministry was a bit overwhelming.

> Can a homeschool mom manage a time-consuming volunteer ministry and continue to care well for her family?
>
> What are the issues I need to be aware of?
>
> In what ways might my return to Young Life negatively impact me or my family?
>
> Would it be wise for me to step back into the ministry at this stage in my life?

My husband and I talked and prayed over these questions again and again. Still, I had no peace about the decision.

So I submitted a request for a wisdom council.

I was asked to e-mail a description of what I was seeking wisdom for. I hit "send," launching my heart's anxious worries off into cyberspace. A couple days later I received word from the lovely couple who lead this ministry. They cc'd me in a note that read:

> Dear Wisdom Council participant,
>
> Thank you for your willingness to participate in the Marina Wallis Wisdom Council. The following is a brief synopsis of Marina's need for input. We will need to pray and consider how we can help Marina come to a decision. See you Sunday, August 26th, at 1:30 in the church conference room.
>
> Dennis & Janis

As I read the names of those who would gather for my council, a twenty-foot-high wave of unworthiness crashed over me. Pastor Joe would be attending, along with his wife, along with five other incredibly God-fearing people whom I deeply respected at our church!

The feelings surfaced again as I walked into our church conference room that Sunday afternoon. Here were nine highly gifted and effective people who had carved out time from their busy lives for the meeting. There are a hundred other places they could have been. Yet here they were, taking their seats around a conference table—just for me.

I was humbled. But I was also greatly encouraged. Just seeing these dear brothers and sisters seated there spoke volumes of love to me. Their presence meant that I—and my decision—really mattered.

Dennis and Janis, the facilitators, opened the meeting in prayer. Introductions followed, and I was asked to share about my situation. Interaction during the next couple hours was rather informal. Council members asked questions, I answered, and they spoke into my situation.

It was unlike anything I had ever encountered at Sunday church or in a small group Bible study. In our small groups at OCF, we pray for one another, and we do pray for issues like the one I was facing. But the wisdom council was a very different experience, since it involved two hours of uninterrupted interaction focused solely upon the nut-and-bolts of my decision about Young Life.

Nine people were fully engaged, fully listening, fully thinking with me about all facets of a topic that had consumed me for quite some time. I recall feeling a bit vulnerable and raw. This was the first time I had let people enter into an area of my life that for months I had contemplated on my own.

The council was a moving experience for me. Brothers and sisters in Christ offered me the gift of attentive listening and wise counsel, in order to help me navigate this challenging crossroad. Never before had I more profoundly felt that the church is a family.

Truth be told, I was hoping the council would tell me what to do. I wanted someone just to make the decision for me. But as the minutes of the meeting ticked by, it became apparent that no one was going to tell me whether or not I should return to Young Life. Instead, they gave me the gift of being equipped with the wisdom I needed to make the very best, sensible, God-honoring decision.

Somewhere along the way my feelings of guilt for taking up all these dear folks' time was replaced with deep gratitude for their willingness to participate in my life. I realized that these brothers and sisters in Christ cared for me. They wouldn't have agreed to be here if it hadn't been for their love of a member of a church who felt burdened. Yes, I still had a big decision ahead of me. But I now felt at peace.

When I heard the facilitator ask, "Do you feel like your needs have been met?" I nodded my head as my eyes welled with tears. God had lavished me with His love through these nine brothers and sisters. My church had become my family. I would never again have to face a major life decision alone.

In the five years that have passed since my wisdom council, I have had the privilege of being on the other end of the ministry, as a council member helping others unpack their difficult life decisions. Giving wisdom to others has built up my faith just as much as being on the receiving end in my own wisdom council. It has been an immense privilege and honor to participate in a ministry that provides a place of rest for the weary members of our church.

Individuals who request a wisdom council genuinely desire to explore the pros, cons, and possible outcomes of a major decision, gleaning insight from the experiences of others. But most do not know quite what to expect at the gathering. Some have toiled with a decision for so long that they do not really expect to hear anything new. Others come hoping to have the decision made for them. Still others simply need to hear "You are still a good Christian if you do this," as they weigh a "tough love" decision against the teachings of Scripture.

Something much bigger and more important inevitably occurs, as the Spirit of the Lord manifests His presence in these councils. Through the testimonies and life experiences of those who sit on the council, the person seeking wisdom is reminded in a profound way that God provides when we depend on Him, and that He is always present and in control of our lives—no matter what decision we make, and no matter what the outcomes of those decisions.

Within a two-hour window, God delivers peace to those who are burdened. He utilizes a council of His people to speak volumes of how deeply He cares for His children and the decisions they face. All because we as His people ask for the wisdom He has promised to give generously.[2]

Finding My Place In God's Story: Rebekah's Pilgrimage in the Arts

Each August the Hellermans spend several weeks vacationing in the mountains, in Mammoth Lakes, California. One afternoon, on one of our getaways, our oldest daughter, then thirteen years old, came out of her room with a play she had written.

---

2. Marina and Joe extend a warm thank-you to Dennis and Janis Bice. Dennis and Janis oversee OCF's wisdom council ministry and attend every meeting. Marina spent time brainstorming with Dennis and Janis in order to craft the first-person account above.

Rebekah has always been into drama. She had participated in a number of children's theater productions at our previous church. On the home front, Rebekah recruited neighborhood friends and staged backyard plays before a captive audience of indulgent parents.

Now she had written a full-length Christmas play. In August.

Developmental psychologists tell us that healthy persons are generally those who have acquired a sense of industry and competency during late childhood and early adolescence. What we discover about our abilities during our early teenage years creates a foundation for our meaning and purpose as adults. The unfortunate alternative is "the feeling that one will never be any good."[3]

This "sense of being useful," as Erik Erikson described it, has a significant social component.[4] As Les Steele rightly observes, "People who feel as if they have something to offer a group will feel as if they belong to it."[5] In this regard, the response of Rebekah's faith community to her Christmas play proved to be a watershed moment in her vocational and spiritual development.

The play was actually kind of cute. Corny, but cute. Margy, our worship leader, who joins us in Mammoth each year, read the script and liked it. The following week she passed it on to one of our pastors. Duke said, "Let's do this thing. It can be our Christmas program this year."

Rebekah recruited kids to play the parts. Margy turned the story into a musical with eight wonderful songs tailored to fit the range and musical abilities of the children. Guided by Margy and our children's director, Rebekah organized the rehearsal schedule and directed her play. At a Sunday morning service in mid-December, Rebekah's dream came to life.

On This Night was hardly a professional undertaking. The kids sang in and out of tune and, of course, they butchered their lines here and there. But the play was meaningful. Rebekah and her cast were beaming. And the church absolutely loved it.

The following year on vacation Rebekah came out of her room with another play. And then another the summer after that.

For four years, during high school, Rebekah wrote and directed OCF's Christmas program. The productions got better and better, as the kids grew in their acting and singing skills, and in their confidence in front of an

---

3. Erickson, *Identity and the Life Cycle*, 92.
4. Ibid., 91.
5. Steele, *On the Way*, 142.

audience. What began as the lone creative exercise of a thirteen-year-old kid had become an annual church tradition.

Then Rebekah went away to college at Biola University and could no longer run the fall rehearsals. With no play and no director, OCF's fledgling Christmas tradition was no more. But Rebekah would never forget how God used her in the lives of those kids.

Biola University had no theater major at the time, so Rebekah majored in education. When she finished her student teaching, she had a job waiting for her at a local grammar school.

But Rebekah had other plans. "I want to start a non-profit academy of the arts that stages plays for kids and young people. My vision is to build character through the arts, based on Judeo-Christian values."

The pragmatist in me was a bit troubled that my daughter was about to turn down a teaching job in a great school district for an entrepreneurial adventure of questionable fiscal viability. But the timing was right. Rebekah was done with school, she was single, and she was financially debt-free. We invited her to move back home for a while to see if she could get her academy off the ground.

Now in its tenth year, Haven Academy of the Arts currently stages four large yearly productions involving several hundred children. The academy also runs theater camps during the summer and has launched another branch at a sister church in inner-city Los Angeles. A production of *Little Women* that Rebekah directed through an adult arm of Haven was chosen by Broadway World as one of the ten best plays in Los Angeles in 2013.

Haven Academy gainfully employs not only Rebekah but her sister, Rachel, as well, along with several part-time staff. The academy ministers to both Christian and non-Christian families. Our church auditorium serves as the venue for the children's plays. Rebekah brings more unchurched families into our facility during a single Haven Academy production than we see on site all the rest of the year.

A little church believed in a little girl and the rest is history.

Some Reflections on a Daughter's Pilgrimage

As a grateful father reflecting back with no little wonder on my daughter's pilgrimage, I am reminded of several providential factors without which Rebekah's vision would not have become a reality. Perhaps most significant was the size of our church at the time.

Why We Need the Church to Become More Like Jesus

OCF now has around six hundred Sunday attenders. We are much too large to give an entire church service over to an unprofessional theater production directed by a high school kid. The expectations of our people are just too high.

When Rebekah was in high school, OCF was a church of about 150. A church this size is less formal and more willing to indulge the dreams of a creative teenager. A small church is also virtually forced to function intergenerationally. As it turned out, this was the most significant factor of all.

Margy, our worship director, and Christy, OCF's children's director, poured themselves into Rebekah. And Rebekah poured herself into the kids in her cast. Parents and children from a dozen church families spent hours and hours together every November, painting sets, figuring out sound and lighting, and designing costumes. Two OCF pastors had children in the plays, so Duke and I, along with our wives, were regularly present to provide direction and encouragement, as well.

Rebekah benefited greatly from the mentoring. And there was a bit of a learning curve in the earlier years. At one rehearsal she became exasperated with her sister and addressed her with one of those "use-this-only-at-home" nicknames (and not when mom and dad are around).

"Hey, Butt-face!" Rebekah hollered at Rachel, right in front of a couple dozen primary-aged church kids playing supporting roles in the play. Oops! No worries. Rebekah apologized, parents were satisfied, and rehearsals continued on schedule.

Many of the relationships Rebekah developed with older adults and younger children continue to this day. One in particular deserves mention. Uncle Bob is a single man in our church who is now in his late seventies.

With a prior interest in theater, Bob proved to be a big fan of the Christmas plays. Uncle Bob became the cast photographer. When she finished college and launched her academy, Bob served as one of Rebekah's board members and oversaw Haven Academy's finances. Over the years Bob has been my daughters' foremost cheerleader in their love for theater. One summer Bob took both Rebekah and Rachel to New York, all expenses paid, for several days, so they could view some top-rate Broadway productions.

Several years ago a marquee on a church a few blocks from my home proclaimed, "What *You* Are Makes Us What *We* Are." How flattering! It's all about me and what I bring to the party.

Not in Rebekah's case. For her we ought to put up a sign in front of OCF that reads, "What *We* Are Makes *You* What You Are."

Rebekah found her place in God's story—and she has matured in Christ—because she was relationally embedded in a healthy intergenerational church family of individuals who could speak into her life and help to make her dreams come true.

Intergenerational Christian Formation

We are spiritually formed in community. But not just any community will do. The section heading above is taken from the title of a recent book by Holly Allen and Christine Ross, which makes a strong case for ministry across the generations.[6]

Large churches generally offer specific programs to meet the changing needs of persons of various ages and interests. Unfortunately, these life-stage ministries tend to isolate the generations from one another in ways that potentially compromise the spiritual progress of the individuals involved.

Allen and Ross remind us that our attraction to life-stage ministries owes more to the influence of culture than to patterns we see in the Bible. We send our children off to school. We go to work. We place aging parents in retirement communities. The result is a trio of mutually isolating social settings for the three generations—not unlike the life-stage ministries operating in many of our churches.

In traditional societies such as the New Testament world, the generations shared life together. This was true of the natural family and it was true of the church family. The early Christians did not have the luxury of life-stage ministry. It would have made little sense to them anyway.

For various reasons, my daughters never connected with OCF's youth ministry. They preferred to spend their time at church serving in the children's department or working in the drama ministry discussed above. In both contexts the girls naturally interacted with people of all ages and from all walks of life.

Rebekah and Rachel remain closely connected to their OCF family. Both of them jumped right back into church life and ministry when they returned from their four years at the university. By contrast, some of the

---

6. Allen and Ross, *Intergenerational Christian Formation*.

kids who were immersed in OCF's high school ministry when my daughters were teenagers no longer walk with the Lord.

Why did Rebekah and Rachel retain their commitment to their church family, while certain others from our youth group did not? The reasons are manifold, but the intergenerational relationships my daughters have enjoyed over the years surely played a part. Indeed, throughout our church, the young adults that have remained faithful to Jesus are generally persons who, like Rebekah and Rachel, had a network of relationships with church members of different ages and interests during their high school years.

I am not opposed to life-stage ministry. Gatherings for mothers of preschoolers, divorce-recovery workshops, parenting courses, and student ministries meet pressing needs in timely ways. Recent research seems to suggest, however, that in our current social context life-stage programming has lasting power only when it functions as an auxiliary arm of a church whose primary orientation toward ministry and spiritual formation is intergenerational.

Spiritual Formation, Community, and the Social Construction of Knowledge

Social scientists increasingly emphasize the role of a community in establishing and reinforcing the religious convictions of its members. A brief discussion of the sociology of knowledge will help us to see why.

Epistemology is the branch of philosophy that wrestles with how we know things. Postmodernity has generated a great degree of epistemological pessimism where religious knowledge is concerned. We are told that there is no such thing as objective religious truth. Each community creates its own religious truth and then socializes its members to adopt it.

Since we have no access to secure knowledge about God (assuming such a Being even exists), each culture must construct its own view of the divine. And since "what is perceived as 'true' within each sub-system or peer-group is bounded by an 'ugly ditch' of epistemological incommensurability," the world's religions are inevitably mutually contradictory in their truth claims.[7]

Knowledge—specifically, religious knowledge (as well as morality and social convictions related to family and gender)—is socially constructed.

---

7. Thiselton, "Signs of the Times," 30.

And, human nature being what it is, the vast majority of us are easily convinced to adopt the views of our social world. It works like this:

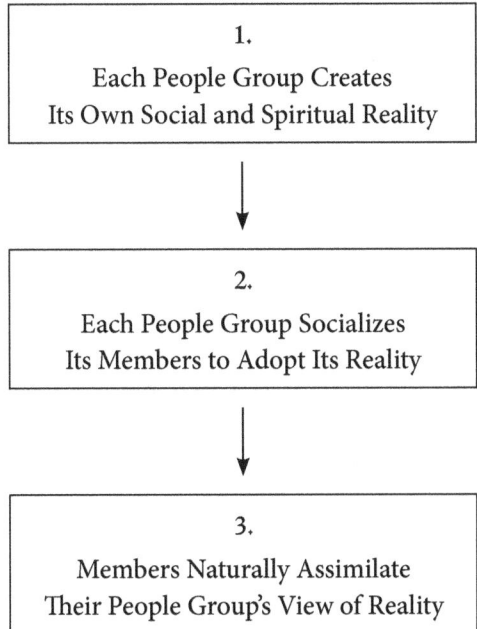

This explains why my daughters are Christian. They were born into a Christian family that is deeply invested in a Christian community. If they had been raised in a Muslim village in the Middle East, they would have been socialized to embrace Islam instead.

When I first became a Christian, in 1975, I attended a basic theology class led by our pastor. The book we used is still in print today: *Decide for Yourself: A Theological Workbook*, by Gordon R. Lewis. According to findings from the sociology of knowledge, the title is misleading. None of us decides for himself or herself. Decisions about life's big questions are made for us by others, before we are even aware that they are being made.

There is something to be said for a pessimistic epistemology where religious knowledge is concerned. After all, how could finite, material human beings ever hope to apprehend the infinite spirit being we call God?

We cannot. The chasm is too great. It is hardly surprising that our attempts to do so have resulted in mutually exclusive religious constructs. Even the Bible asserts, "No one has ever seen God" (John 1:18a), because from our side, as finite creatures, no one can. The truth about God had to come from the Other side.

And it did, preeminently in the incarnation of God the Son: "the only God, who is at the Father's side, he has made him known" (John 1:18b). "Whoever has seen me has seen the Father" (John 14:9). The biblical claims about Jesus—historically authenticated by his resurrection from the dead—put the lie to any epistemological project that would dismiss all religious knowledge as socially constructed.

So much for extreme epistemological pessimism where religious truth is concerned. The statement in box 1 above must be qualified by what God has chosen to reveal about himself in the Bible, in creation, and, finally and fully, in the incarnation of God the Son.

Postmodern thinking about community socialization, reflected in boxes 2 and 3, is another story entirely. Here we have much to learn.

Social theorists such as Peter Berger and Thomas Luckmann view communities as "plausibility structures" that reinforce a group's core convictions in the minds of its members.[8] Christian Smith applies this thinking to religious communities: "Religion survives and can thrive in a pluralistic, modern society by embedding itself in subcultures that offer satisfying morally orienting collective identities which provide adherents meaning and belonging."[9] This is all quite biblical. Paul warned the Corinthians, "Do not be deceived: Bad company ruins good morals," and, we may assume, good theology (1 Cor 15:33).

I never cease to be amazed by parents who tell me that they are unwilling to impose their spiritual convictions on their children because they want them to make their own decisions about religion. They send their kids off to school—first the public schools, then the best university they can afford—so that their children can learn to think for themselves.

No one thinks for himself. Every high school campus and every university—public or private—is a community with a dominant, defining, circumscribed view of reality. And that includes religious reality. Peer relationships on a high school campus, and power relations between esteemed professors and lowly students at the university, virtually guarantee that our children will be socialized to assimilate the belief structures and moral priorities

---

8. Berger and Luckmann, *Social Construction of Reality*, 157; Berger, *Rumor of Angels*, 34–37. See, more recently, Hjelm, *Social Constructionisms*, 17–36.

9. Smith, *American Evangelicalism*, 118.

of these communities—unless, that is, they are simultaneously confronted with the influence of another, more compelling, community.

Our foray into postmodern epistemology is not unrelated to my daughters' experience at OCF. What we have learned about community socialization goes a long way to explain why some teenagers stick with church while others do not.

Some communities are simply more powerful and ultimately more effective than others in socializing their members to adopt their worldview. This is a crucial observation.

There was a time when a well-executed youth ministry offered a community socialization experience that could compete with anything the world had to offer. Back in the 1970s and 1980s, when I was involved in youth work, life-stage programs targeting high-schoolers and college students played a central role in establishing and reinforcing deep Christian convictions among our young people during their formative years.

This is no longer the case. Not only has the surrounding culture become less and less Christian. The nearly irresistible socializing influence of pagan youth culture now confronts our teenagers 24/7 through social media. Even while they are sitting in church.

It's Wednesday night in the youth room. Josh, the high school pastor, passionately exhorts his teenagers to remain sexually pure until marriage. Sam, in the back row, scrolls through images of a scantily clad pop star on his smartphone. Sam will probably not attend church at all a few years from now. Research by the Barna Group finds 59 percent of millennials (born between 1984 and 2012) leaving church permanently, or for an extended period, during the first decade of their adult life.[10]

The Barna Group cites a number of reasons for the exodus. More interesting in the present connection, however, are the reasons that the other 41 percent choose to stay. Apparently, God's people still have the resources to provide a community experience whose power to socialize its members rivals anything the world can throw at us.

As it turns out, "the most positive church experiences among Millennials are relational."[11] But not just any relationship will do.

Intergenerational relationships topped the list of reasons that young people remain connected to their faith communities. Those who stayed,

---

10. The data cited in the following paragraphs is taken from Barna Group, "5 Reasons."

11. Ibid.

in Barna's study, were twice as likely to have a close personal friendship with an adult in the church as those who left (59 percent versus 31 percent). The same was the case for more intentional relationships: 28 percent of Millennials still in the church had an adult mentor, compared to only 11 percent of the dropouts.

Young people also cite purpose and mission as reasons to stay connected. Millennials need to be launched into meaningful ministry now, and not kept waiting until they are grownups, married-with-kids.

Millennials long to find their place in God's story. Those who do are more likely to hang around. Barna found that young adults who have remained active are three times more likely than dropouts to say they learned to view their gifts and passions as part of God's calling (45 percent versus 17 percent).

Meaningful relationships with older adults. Finding our place in God's story. Using our gifts in the church. This all sounds a whole lot like Rebekah Hellerman's experience at OCF.

David Kinnaman puts it all together in a summary of the Barna Group's findings: "Cultivating intergenerational relationships is one of the most important ways in which effective faith communities are developing flourishing faith in both young and old. In many churches, this means changing the metaphor from simply passing the baton to the next generation to a more functional, biblical picture of a body—that is, the entire community of faith, across the entire lifespan, working together to fulfill God's purposes."[12]

Grassroots Community: The Hardies' Sunday Night Adventure

Rebekah found her calling in the context of an organized church ministry, OCF's Christmas production. OCF's wisdom council operates as a church-sponsored program as well. It is often the case, however, that our most meaningful community experiences do not come about formally, through the vision of a pastor or at weekly events on the church calendar. They arise, rather, from grassroots efforts by individuals in the congregation who long for more than traditional church programming tends to provide.

Eric and Jeannie Hardie and their daughters epitomize the ideal of a natural family that is deeply embedded in their faith family, across the

12. Ibid.

Rooted in the Family of God

generations. Eric is a professional writer for Mattel Incorporated, so I will let Eric tell his family's story about an informal community from our church that the Hardies host on Sunday evenings.

I push through the front door carrying a 40-pound case of raw chicken wings and set it on the counter next to kitchen sink. My wife, Jeannie, looks up from her computer and asks,

"How many are coming over tonight?"

I mentally tick through the list of those who've responded and arrive at forty—not counting the possibility of a walk in or four. Fried chicken does seem to resonate strongly with our group.

"Shall I warn the neighbors or alert the National Guard?" Jeannie asks.

"Since 15 of the 40 are kids, probably both," I reply.

To her credit Jeannie doesn't bat an eye. It's our community, after all.

I was about to say that this community of ours started a short few years ago with a single young married couple arriving on Sundays at 5:30 PM for dinner for a few hours of fellowship around the table. In truth though, the seeds of the gathering were planted in our childhood.

Jeannie and I both grew up in large extended southern families. Community, as we experienced it, consisted of grandparents, aunts, uncles, and cousins (lots of cousins) all concentrated within a small geographical area easily traversed, more or less, on a tank of gas. Visits were usually announced by arrival, and no one dropped in who didn't stay long enough to catch up on the latest family news or share an opinion about current events in the world around us. Adding our church communities to the mix meant the idea of "alone time" was as foreign to us as store-bought tomatoes.

Our parents taught us the basics of what they thought we needed to know. The extended family then filled in any gaps of knowledge they thought perhaps our parents might have left out. Sometimes mom and dad responded to this new information with knowing nods of approval. Other times it resulted in looks of shock and disbelief, followed by private conversations with the particular family sage who had disseminated said revelation.

When Jeannie and I think back on those times, the conversations we recall with the utmost clarity and fondness are the ones that occurred while the extended family gathered around a meal. There is something about breaking bread together in a communal setting that goes well beyond simply supplying the body's need for physical nourishment. It creates an atmosphere that bonds people together like nothing else.

Rarely have I ever witnessed good food engender genuine animosity between those sharing it together. And never is the spirit of hospitality more on display than when the only expected payback from the fruits of someone's labor in the kitchen consists of full plates, second helpings, and empty serving dishes when the meal is over.

Jeannie and I met in graduate school in Virginia, and it was the shared experiences of our intergenerational, extended-family upbringings that helped our relationship develop. We married after I graduated, and a year later we moved to Los Angeles so I could pursue a screenwriting career.

Out of the three million or so people who live here, we knew exactly two of them well enough to have their phone numbers. When we finally found an apartment we could afford, it was nowhere near either of the two. Nevertheless, it was an exciting time in a young couple's life. We were hopeful that I would quickly find a writing job and that we would find a community to share life with.

It didn't take long for reality to set in. I soon found out that screenwriting jobs were as scarce as snow days in Southern California. And although people weren't unfriendly, they were constantly on the move with little time for new arrivals.

That first year was difficult. We were buffeted by a seemingly endless set of waves, including a life-threatening medical emergency. And then there was that series of automotive adventures involving, among other things, an attempted theft of one vehicle that left it disabled, a successful theft of another, and what seemed to be an invisible "Please Crash Into Me" sign on every car and truck we drove.

Our apartment was bordered by Korea Town on one side and a large Hispanic neighborhood on the other, which made finding a local church with services in English difficult. We were driving an hour each way to attend church with one friend we knew, but trying to commute through Los Angeles traffic for community-building activities during the week became an exercise in frustration if not futility.

Our first year in California was a lonely time. There were moments when we felt absolutely helpless without the support of a community around us.

By God's grace we made it through. And we were now determined to do whatever we could to provide a safe haven of community for others coming to LA who needed it. Little did we know that this determination would take us from being a married couple, alone in the big city, to breaking bread with forty adults and children from our church family nearly every Sunday night.

It began in our one-bedroom apartment. In the three years we lived there, no less than ten different people came through the door to sleep on our

Rooted in the Family of God

couch for various lengths of time. Some we knew well. Others, who found us through word of mouth from mutual friends, we didn't know at all.

Three years later we were able to buy the 1,500 square-foot, two-bedroom house we live in today. When we signed the papers, Jeannie and I told the Lord that our door would never be closed to anyone who needed a place to stay or a meal to eat. The Lord has been faithful in sending folks our way, and we've done our best to make sure the door always swings wide.

After we settled into our new home, we began to look for a church, a process that I rank right up there with shopping for a new car. (Overenthusiastic people in ill-fitting suits trying to sell me something I don't want or need give me the shivers.) Fortunately for us—actually more fortunate for Jeannie, who dislikes the steeple chase more than I do—the second church we took for a test drive was OCF.

A visitor that day wore the only suit in sight, and the enthusiasm of the regular attenders seemed to flow from a place of genuine affection for each other. It wasn't long before we were involved in a small group and met a family who invited us to join their Sunday night dinner community. We began as friends, but over the next eight years of Sunday nights we became family. But life, and the Lord in his timing, has a way of moving us all on, and so we all did.

We had become parents during this time, and one of the things we began to miss, aside from the food and fellowship, was the opportunity for our two daughters to be in the company of other adults in our church family.

When Jeannie and I were growing up, the communal meals provided a rare chance for us to listen in on adult conversations (often more interesting than chitchat with our peers) without being shooed away. It was an important part of learning how to respectfully listen, ask questions, and build relationships across the generations.

Jeannie was especially impacted by watching the men in her community conduct themselves with character and integrity. She said their example kept her from "marrying a jerk"—her words not mine. As parents, we began to long for our girls to experience this kind of extended-family upbringing. So we decided to start our own small community.

Ms. Krista and Mr. Bobby, the young couple mentioned above, became a Sunday night fixture, followed a few weeks later by Mr. Craig, Ms. Ann and their son Eli. We had a nice group of nine people and never expected it to go much beyond that.

The Lord had other plans.

Why We Need the Church to Become More Like Jesus

"Hey! I hear you guys are doing dinner on Sunday nights. Can we come?"

Word of mouth had spread, probably from Craig, who is a deputy district attorney and talks for a living. At any rate, we figured that another family or two wouldn't be that big a deal.

Soon, though, a single package of paper plates, knives, and forks wasn't enough, and it was taking more than a couple of casual conversations to tell people what I was cooking and what they should bring to go with it.

The numbers didn't overwhelm us as much as the desire. There was a hunger—pun intended—for a kind of informal community with no agenda other than what was on the menu for the night. Eventually, a Facebook group had to be created as an information hub for Sunday Night Dinner.

Actually, "information hub" makes it sound far more logistical then it really is. Most of the time I post on Friday (sometimes Saturday) something along the lines of, "Tacos OK with everybody?" or "Cooking some cut of beef. Please bring sides accordingly."

Sometimes the group is large. Sometimes it's small. We figure that the Lord knows who needs to be here and prompts hearts accordingly. A few people in the group actually give us a heads-up on what they're going to bring. A few others ask what they should bring. But we never really know what dinner will look like until people show up. I fully expect that one night we'll have nine bowls of macaroni and cheese, a green salad, and hominy—in which case I have promised to post pictures on our Facebook site.

A word to anyone who wants to start something like this. Community is messy. Your sink will get piled high with dishes left for you to clean, your floors will get tracked on with dirt, kids will hide plates of leftovers in places your nose will discover before your eyes do, and your neighbors will start to look at you with a mixture of wonder and fear.

Beyond the food-related messiness is the messiness of the lives you will touch. Hospitality is a beacon for those who need it, and your guests will often come with more than a hunger for food. Be prepared for those times when someone asks if they can come early or stay late to "talk to you about something."

Here are a few more things we've learned. Let others in the group help if they ask, because they want to be invested in their community as well. Neither should you be afraid to take a night off every once in a while. Our Sunday gathering is not a weekly program on a church calendar, and it has not hurt our community at all to skip an evening now and then. Our people understand.

And don't waste valuable time trying to sanitize every corner of your house. All this will do is rob you of joy by turning the preparations for your community adventure into a chore. Your folks already know you have dust balls, and they obviously don't care, 'cause they continue to show up every Sunday!

Finally (I speak as the cook for our gatherings), if you plan for ten people and twenty show up, don't panic. You can always make pancakes (yes, for Sunday dinner) or stall for a half-hour until the pizza arrives. Allow the Lord to bring who he wills into your community. Whether it's four, forty, or four hundred, if we provide a willing heart, the Lord is pretty good about taking care of the rest. Speaking of 40...

A high-pitched "Waaaaaaah!" interrupts the squeals of laughter and play coming from the fifteen children in the front yard. It's also the only sound that can cut through the boisterous conversation of the twenty-five adults inside.

The front door opens. Offender and offended appear to plead their cases. The respective parents patiently sort out all the "he-said" and "she-said." Tears are dried, apologies issued, and play and conversation resume. It's a picture of our Sunday night community in a nutshell: rarely quiet, sometimes serious, and always messy—joyously messy.

Thank you, Eric. I hope you know that the relational blessings of your Sunday night community overflow into the life and culture of our broader church family. I see this as your pastor. And I have experienced it firsthand as a father.

I do not attend Eric and Jeannie's Sunday night adventure, but one of my daughters became involved several years ago as a single adult in her late twenties. While she was part of the Hardies' community, Rebekah began a serious dating relationship. Matt seemed like a solid Christian guy, but he was not part of our church family. No one at OCF (except Rebekah's sister, Rachel) knew him very well.

Rebekah wisely wanted to observe her potential mate interacting with the people she knew the best. One Sunday night she brought Matt to the Hardies'.

After some brief introductions, Rebekah left Matt out in the backyard to fend for himself with the cigar-smoking "boys," so that the men in Rebekah's life could vet this new boyfriend and see what he was made of. Word has it that Craig, the Assistant DA, gave Matt quite the runaround.

Matt apparently passed the test with flying colors. It is now three years later, and Matt and Rebekah will soon celebrate their second wedding anniversary.

As the Hardies' pastor, I am thankful for the meaningful community experience that Eric and Jeannie provide for so many of our people. It is a model I would like to see replicated throughout our church.

As Rebekah's father, I am profoundly grateful to Eric and Jeannie Hardie that my daughter did not have to negotiate the challenge of finding a mate on her own. It meant all the world to Joann and me to see Rebekah's future husband affirmed by those dear brothers and sisters in Christ who had come to know and love our daughter through the Hardies' Sunday-night community.

Here is a final postscript related to the Hardies and their commitment to the values you are reading about in this book.[13] Like most young couples, Eric and his wife Jeannie, faced quite a challenge with the overpriced Southern California housing market. They finally settled on the home Eric mentioned above, in a less-than-ideal neighborhood, where the school system is marginal, and where the average price for a small single-family house is still about four hundred thousand dollars.

Several years ago, Hasbro, a multinational toy and board game company, offered Eric a once-in-a-lifetime job opportunity that came with a significant salary increase. Hasbro's headquarters are located in Pawtucket, Rhode Island, where two hundred thousand dollars buys a family a nice three- or four-bedroom home. The schools rate significantly higher than those in the Hardies' current neighborhood as well.

A move to New England would have been a big win for the Hardie family. Most couples would have enthusiastically accepted the job and relocated their family.

Eric and Jeannie declined the offer. The Hardies are deeply embedded in their church family and could not imagine life without the relationships they have cultivated during their years at OCF.

Priorities like these pay deep spiritual and relational dividends. I believe that Eric and Jeannie would tell you that their family is healthier as a result of their decision to stay. And because of their long tenure, Eric and Jeannie are highly influential in the lives of others at OCF, both formally

---

13. The next few paragraphs first appeared in an article in *Christianity Today*: http://www.christianitytoday.com/ct/2016/august-web-only/if-our-families-are-more-important-than-our-churches-we-nee.html?start=1/.

(in the areas of spiritual formation and the arts) and informally (in settings like their Sunday night dinners).

While we may not be faced with a decision to relocate, many of us prioritize natural family in more subtle ways. Many of us keep our families so busy that little time remains to develop the kinds of relationships God intends for his faith family. Perhaps it is time to reorient our calendars around the priorities of the family of God.

Conclusion

Strong-group church is not a transferable program that we can take from church to church like some kind of Sunday school curriculum. But neither is New Testament community just another impractical ideal that cannot thrive in the radically different cultural soil of American evangelical church life.

The above narratives clearly demonstrate that we can in fact recapture Jesus's vision for authentic Christian community in our churches today. I trust that the stories about (a) OCF's wisdom council ministry, (b) Rebekah's pilgrimage in the arts, and (c) Eric and Jeannie Hardies' Sunday gathering have given you a feeling for what can happen when God's children are relationally rooted in a healthy church family.

It is not easy to make the shift from church as we know it to community as experienced by the early Christians. And the above stories might be a bit misleading along these lines, because they may have given you the impression that the people at OCF really get this strong-group community stuff. After all, one of its teaching pastors, Joe Hellerman, is an expert of sorts on the social history of early Christianity, and he has written a half dozen books on the subject. How could OCF not be a fully functioning strong-group community?

Very easily, I am sad to say. Of the six hundred or so attenders on any given Sunday, I estimate that about one hundred of them are deeply embedded in our church family, living out the strong-group values outlined in the first chapters of this book. And that is a generous estimate.

Challenging the pervasive individualism and consumerism of our culture continues to be a daunting task. OCF could probably do a much better job of it than we currently do.

Yet I remain encouraged, because I am convinced that God is on the side of those who pursue the kind of relational Christianity illustrated above. Stories like these remind us that the Holy Spirit stands ready to work in remarkable ways in the lives of individuals and churches who are committed to seeing God's church become the community Jesus intends it to be.

5

How We Lost Our Way

The Evangelical Journey from "Us" to "Me"

> Be more splendid. Be more extraordinary.
> Use every moment to fill yourself up.
>
> —Oprah Winfrey

> We have trained Christians to be demanding consumers, not disciples.
>
> —Kent Carlson and Mike Lueken[1]

BY THE END OF the twentieth century, Western individualism had established itself as a formidable influence among American evangelicals. A 1998 study by George Barna found that American Christians

- prefer a variety of church experiences rather than getting the most out of all that a single church has to offer.
- think that spiritual enlightenment comes from diligence in a discovery process, rather than from commitment to a faith community and perspective.
- view religion as a commodity that we consume, rather than one in which we invest ourselves.

David R. Nienhuis, writing a decade later, summarizes the present state of affairs: "Many American consumer-congregants have come to expect their churches to function as communities of goods and services that provide

---

1. Carlson and Lueken, *Renovation of the Church*, 85. See pp. 64–73 for Carlson's insightful discussion of the negative effects of consumerism on American church life.

care and comfort without the kind of challenge and discipline required for authentic Christian formation to take place."[2] This consumerist preoccupation with personal faith experience contrasts sharply with the community-oriented mindset of early Christianity reflected in the biblical metaphors of the body of Christ (chapter 1) and the family of God (chapter 2). What has caused this profound departure from the faith of our fathers?

A thorough analysis of the long and complex journey from "Us" (collectivism) to "Me" (individualism) in Western society, and its effect upon Christian theology, is beyond the scope of this project.[3] It will prove helpful, however, to carefully consider several ways radical individualism has compromised biblical truth in recent decades in American church life. The first relates to the way in which evangelicals frame the gospel.

Have Your Heard of *The Four Spiritual Laws?*— Personal Evangelism (1970s)

When I became a follower of Jesus in 1975, churches placed great emphasis on sharing our faith through personal evangelism. It was the era of Evangelism Explosion and the gospel tract.

For several summers, the singles group I pastored spent a weekend camping at Jalama Beach, California. We did a whole lot of eating, enjoyed some outdoor sports (Jalama has some of central California's best surf), and held a meeting or two. We also canvassed the campground, sharing *The Four Spiritual Laws* with anyone who would listen.

The Four Spiritual Laws was the most popular gospel tract during the heyday of personal evangelism. It may very well be the most widely distributed religious booklet in history, with 2.5 billion copies printed in 144 languages, as of 2013. Since Bill Bright wrote the tract in 1952, God has mightily used *The Four Spiritual Laws* to lead countless individuals to faith.

No evangelistic tool is perfect, however, and it is quite clear, in retrospect, that American individualism has significantly shaped the presentation of the gospel in *The Four Spiritual Laws*. The tract is not biblically

---

2. Nienhuis, "Problem of Biblical Illiteracy," 12.

3. For the influence of Western individualism on the American cultural landscape, consult the engaging works of Bellah et al., *Habits of the Heart*; and Putnam, *Bowling Alone*. Individualism as we know it finds its origins in late medieval Europe. See, for example, Morris, *Discovery of the Individual*.

inaccurate. Rather it is the booklet's emphasis—not its theological content—that I want us to consider.

The Four Spiritual Laws focuses almost exclusively upon what God has in store for the individual rather than upon the encompassing narrative of creation, fall, redemption, and restoration that we encounter in Scripture. The anthropocentric orientation (my story versus God's story) runs throughout the tract. Law 1 states, "God loves you and offers you a wonderful plan for your life." Law 4 assures us that "we can know and experience God's plan for our lives."

The "Me" orientation of The four laws becomes particularly problematic when we search the tract for any evidence of the concern for "us," so central to early Christianity. On page 15 (of fifteen and a half total pages) readers are finally encouraged to "Fellowship In a Good Church."[4] The placement of the exhortation at the end of the tract, appended to an alliterated list of "Six Suggestions for Christian G.R.O.W.T.H."—implies that the church is a necessary but utilitarian afterthought, existing only to help the individual believer mature in personal relationship with Jesus.

The New Testament notion that we are saved to community—and deeply dependent on the local church for our spiritual development—fails to see the light of day in *The Four Spiritual Laws*.

Two Ways to Frame the Gospel

There is another, more subtle way that gospel tracts like *The Four Spiritual Laws* reinforce an unbiblical individualism in our thinking about Christian faith and practice.

The pastors at OCF recently worked our way through Tim Keller's *Center Church*, a book brimming with helpful insights for local church leaders. Particularly illuminating is Keller's discussion of the contextualization the gospel.

Keller outlines two approaches. The first, the systematic theological method (STM), takes a topical, synchronic approach to Scripture, organizing biblical truth thematically. Rightly assuming the unity of the Scriptures, the STM gathers together everything the Bible says on a given topic. Readers acquainted with the systematic theologies of Wayne Grudem and Millard Erickson will find themselves in familiar territory here.

---

4. Based on a current version of Bright, *Four Spiritual Laws*.

In the case of the gospel, the STM generates a series of propositions about God, sin, Christ, and faith—much like *The Four Spiritual Laws* does. The STM emphasizes the *means* of salvation, namely, the work of Christ on the cross and the faith response of the individual. The STM answers the question, *What must I do to be saved?*

Keller labels the second way of framing the gospel the redemptive historical method (RHM). The RHM reads the Bible diachronically, "along its narrative arc." Keller elaborates:

> [The RHM] organizes what the Bible says by stages in history or by the plotline of a story: *The Bible is about God's creating the world, the fall of man, God's reentry into history to create a new people for himself, and eventually about a new creation that emerges out of a marred and broken world through Christ.*[5]

The RHM emphasizes the *purpose* of salvation, a renewed creation. It answers the question, *What hope is there for the world?*

SYSTEMATIC THEOLOGICAL METHOD	REDEMPTIVE HISTORICAL METHOD
Synchronic	Diachronic
Topical	Historical
Propositional	Narrative
Emphasis: The *Means* of Salvation = The Atonement	Emphasis: The *Purpose* of Salvation = New Creation
Answers A "Me" Question: *What must I do to be saved?*	Answers An "Us" Question: *What hope is there for the world?*

Until a decade or so ago, I had never heard the gospel presented as redemptive history. I find it highly encouraging that we are rediscovering God's great story of redemption as outlined in the Bible.

Keller's taxonomy triggered several aha moments as OCF's leaders discussed this portion of *Center Church*. We minister as a team, and several of us rotate through the pulpit. It was immediately apparent to all that Joe Hellerman is the RHM guy on the team.

---

5. Keller, *Center Church*, 40 (italics original).

My PhD is in history, not theology, so it is hardly surprising that I tend to approach Scripture diachronically, as a historical narrative. At the beginning of my sermons I often remind our church family, "The Bible is the story of God fixing the mess we have made of the life he has given us so that he can receive the glory that is his due." I then situate our passage for the morning in its respective place in the unfolding biblical drama.

Keller's twofold schema also explains why evangelicals typically present the gospel the way we do. Although I was hardly sophisticated enough to recognize it at the time, when I first became a Christian I was taught to share the gospel via the systematic theological method. We all were. *The Four Spiritual Laws* is a textbook example of the STM's synchronic, propositional framing of the good news.

The STM has won millions of persons to Christ. It has also reinforced Western individualism in the minds of evangelical Christians, particularly in the markedly anthropocentric form of the method that we encounter in our gospel tracts.

Keller rightly affirms both the STM and the RHM as biblical, orthodox, and necessary. He introduces the distinction not to privilege one approach over the other but rather to show how the respective methods resonate differently in different cultural settings.

It was certainly a stroke of genius for churches and parachurch organizations to leverage the STM to present the gospel to an audience of American individualists during the second half of the twentieth century. The STM addressed the very question that seekers from the baby boomer generation were asking: *What must I do to be saved?* Many found their answer to that question in Jesus, and for that we remain grateful.

The STM answers a "me" question. This in itself is not problematic. The gospel requires that we come to God individually through the atoning work of Christ's death on the cross.

The problem arises when we recast the STM's individualistic framing of the gospel—*What must I do to be saved?*—solely in terms of private spirituality and personal fulfillment: *What must I do to have a wonderful plan for my life?* Christian community is nowhere in view, biblical salvation becomes just another form of self-discovery, and the stage is set for the kind of Christian consumerism that surfaced in the 1998 Barna study outlined at the beginning of the chapter.

A systematic theological framing of the gospel (God–sin–Christ–faith) is orthodox and biblical. Unfortunately, it is too easily hijacked and compromised by the radical individualism of our social context.

The time has come for Western evangelicals to recontextualize the message of salvation in a redemptive historical framework, which emphasizes God's design for all of creation. Perhaps more than ever before, new believers need to learn at the beginning of their Christian lives that the adventure lying ahead of them is primarily about being swept up into God's grand narrative, and only secondarily about a plan that God might have for their individual lives.

I cannot become a follower of Jesus without personally trusting in the atoning work of Christ. Any methodology—whether the STM or RHM—must include this foundational biblical reality in its gospel presentation. But I do not trust in the atoning work of Christ in order to embark upon some "wonderful plan" that God has custom-tailored for my individual life.

To trust in Christ's work on the cross is to abandon myself to play my part in a very different plan, namely, God's marvelous, all-encompassing plan "to bring all things in heaven and on earth together under one head, even Christ" (Eph 1:9–10). There is no plan more wonderful than this.

The RHM may prove timely for other reasons as well. Students with whom I interact at Biola University have become highly sensitive to global challenges related to the environment and social justice. Young people are increasingly looking beyond themselves to ask *What hope is there for the world?* The RHM's answer to this question—a redeemed humanity and a renewed creation—is precisely what our broken world needs to hear.

What Color Is Your Spiritual Parachute?— Spiritual Gifts (1980s)

The spiritual gifts craze also reveals how modern evangelicals have bought into the "me" orientation of our culture. Spiritual gifts became the rage back in the 1980s, when I was working in single adult ministry. It was as if we had found some ancient manuscripts with passages in the Bible that we had never seen before.

Multitudes of sermons were preached from 1 Corinthians 12–14, Ephesians 4, and Romans 12. High-profile pastors gave countless seminars on how to find our spiritual gifts. A think-tank at Fuller Seminary created a Spiritual Gifts Inventory whereby through a series of multiple-choice questions we could each discover our unique and fulfilling ministry in the body of Christ.

Debates arose, quite acrimonious at times, between cessationists and noncessationists over the validity of the "sign-gifts" for the church today. If I recall correctly, the two theological camps even had their own spiritual-gifts profiles, with specific sets of questions designed to reflect their respective views on the issue. The diagnostic inventory I took certainly did not have any questions on it about the so-called miraculous gifts. We could not have a Conservative Baptist Association singles pastor like Joe Hellerman discovering that he had the gift of tongues.

It is easy to see, in retrospect, that the whole enterprise was being driven by a hopelessly anthropocentric preoccupation with personal fulfillment. The spiritual gifts craze of the 1980s was all about the individual Christian finding his or her perfect place in God's ecclesiastical economy or, in the case of some of our more charismatic brothers and sisters, personally experiencing the "fullness" of God.

How could it have been otherwise? For as has been the case with so many trends in American evangelicalism, the church simply jumped on the bandwagon of popular culture, which was at least decade ahead of us in the business of personal fulfillment.

Captivated by a Cultural Trend

In 1970, a book came out called *What Color Is Your Parachute?* It became so popular that it has been updated and republished nearly every year since. The author, Richard Bolles, encourages the reader to pick a career that fits his or her temperament, gifts, aptitude, and abilities, so that work will be a personally satisfying experience, rather than a perennially stultifying nine-to-five grind.

Find out what color your parachute is, pick a career accordingly, and you will be guaranteed a delightfully fulfilling descent through the vocational atmosphere of life, as well as a soft and satisfying landing when you hit the ground.[6]

In the years that followed, vocational psychologists developed an assortment of assessment tools to help us find our place in the workforce. Who among us has not taken DISC or StrengthsQuest?

---

6. Yes, Bolles has even coauthored a book titled *What Color Is Your Parachute? For Retirement,* now in its second edition.

Are you an Achiever, an Investigator, or a Promoter? A Blue, a Green, or a Red? Or are you a messy mix of categories, like me, who tends to find these tools rather frustrating?

I want us to notice two things. First of all, the connection between (a) the spiritual gifts craze in the 1980s and (b) the focus on job satisfaction in the culture at large is hardly coincidental. Just add the appropriate adjective to the title of that 1970 best seller and it all becomes quite clear: *What Color Is Your* Spiritual *Parachute*?

We have simply taken yet another trend from the dominant culture and Christianized it. Sometimes that works, when the trend happens to be a morally neutral one (e.g., certain styles of music or clothing). But can we really Christianize an anthropocentric view of reality, of any stripe?

With age comes perspective, and in this case twenty-twenty hindsight proves rather revealing to this sixty-five-year-old. After more than three decades of hubbub about spiritual gifts and ministerial satisfaction, I find it almost embarrassing to discover that there is not a single word about personal fulfillment in 1 Corinthians 12–14, Ephesians 4, or Romans 12. Not a word.

In contrast, the biblical teaching challenges us to use our gifts to serve one another, to edify the body of Christ in the context of local church ministry—"for the common good," as Paul puts it (1 Cor 12:7).

One of the great ironies of the kingdom is that those who give their lives away in the service of others do in fact discover their spiritual gifts and experience a great deal of fulfillment. However, the pathway to fulfillment in the Christian life is not a pilgrimage of self-discovery. It is a pilgrimage of self-denial:

> If anyone would come after me, let him deny himself and take up his cross and follow me. For whoever would save his life will lose it, but whoever loses his life for my sake and the gospel's will save it. (Mark 8:34–35)

The Anomaly of Personal Fulfillment

A second observation has to do with the cultural anomaly of the whole personal fulfillment rage to begin with, whether it has to do with our careers in the workforce or with our roles in the church.

My father and mother were born in 1903 and 1915, respectively. They lived through two world wars, and both went through the Great Depression. As I was growing up, my dad sold shoes. My mom was a clerk for a lumber company and, later, a drugstore.

What color were my parents' parachutes? The thought never crossed their minds. Why not? Because people in my parents' generation were thankful to have any parachute at all. My dad did not choose to manage a shoe store because he had a special affinity for the smell of leather. And Mom certainly had no meaningful relationship with her adding machine (the 1960s prototype of the MacBook Pro).

As is the case with the great majority of the world's population even today, personal fulfillment was nowhere on my parents' vocational radar screen. They were satisfied simply to have jobs to support our family. Any color parachute will do just fine, thank you.

Only the post–World War II boom of the 1950s and '60s in the West (especially in the U.S.A.) generated the kind of socioeconomic environment in which individuals have had the luxury to choose a vocation that offers the promise of job satisfaction. The idea—so familiar to us—that I should pursue a vocation that matches my gifts and temperament is an anomaly in world history.

Even today in most places around the world a person does not get to choose a vocation. He or she engages in the same kind of subsistence labor that the family has always done. And this has been the case throughout human history. If your dad, Zebedee, is a fisherman, then you had better pick up a net. That is your "parachute," James and John, whether it happens to fit your special gift mix or not (Mark 1:19–20).

What all this means is that the great majority of people on this planet cannot hope to find fulfillment in *what* they do. They must seek fulfillment in the simple fact *that* they do—that is, that they are able to do something, anything, to provide for their families.

This applies to the spiritual arena as well. How many of our brothers and sisters in rural India, for example, get to ponder their particular spiritual gift mix, with the help, of course, of the latest edition of the appropriate diagnostic tools?

The next time someone asks you to take a spiritual gifts test, it might help to remember that Jesus did not say, "Whoever finds his life will save it." If that were the case, a meaningful life on this planet would be available only to those of us who have the luxury to find ourselves, to discover the color of our spiritual parachutes, so to speak, so that we can serve Christ in those areas of ministry that promise to provide immediate personal satisfaction.

God Wants to Meet My Needs:
The Seeker-Sensitive Movement (1990s)

From 1984 to 1990 I was pastor of single adults in a traditional Conservative Baptist Association congregation. The church did an admirable job of sending and supporting cross-cultural missionaries. We were ineffective, however, at reaching our local community with the gospel. Attendance had hovered around five hundred to six hundred since I had come to the church in 1975.

The creative strategies of a new boss changed all that. In 1991 the church hired a senior pastor who had recently earned his Doctor of Ministry degree in the field of church growth.

The preaching changed dramatically. Instead of expository sermons based on a paragraph or chapter in the Bible, we now heard topical messages supported by individual verses taken from assorted Scripture passages. Moreover, the sermons did not address traditional theological categories, such as the holiness of God or the deity of Christ. Instead, they targeted the felt needs of persons in the congregation.

Thousands of flyers were sent out to local residents advertising a sermon series titled Home Improvement, piggy-backing on a TV sitcom with the same title. The mailer sought to provide our neighbors with the hope that God could improve their marriages or help them to raise better kids.

The seeker-sensitive movement had been born. Our new pastor jumped on the bandwagon with abandon. And baby boomers in our trendy beach community responded with such enthusiasm that today the church ministers to well over two thousand people each weekend.

Success is intoxicating, and it took some time for the reservations many of us had about seeker sensitivity to gain much traction. Twenty-five years later the theological bankruptcy of the movement is apparent.

Seeker-sensitive churches brought a me-oriented gospel to a me-oriented culture. The inevitable result? A multitude of me-oriented Christians. Narcissistic baby boomers responded in droves to a gospel that promised them the world. The church became a mile wide and an inch deep. It was a perfect storm theologically.

Two aspects of the movement clashed directly with the biblical view of spirituality and sanctification. Most obvious was an appeal to the consumerist mentality that pervades American society at large.

During the 1990s, Kent Carlson was on the cutting edge of the seeker movement as the pastor of a large and growing church. Reevaluation began when Carlson recognized that by enthusiastically playing into the dynamics of consumerism, church leaders implicitly reinforce an "antibiblical value system": "By harnessing the power of consumerism to grow our churches, *we are more firmly forming our people into consumers.* Pastors end up being as helpful as bartenders at an Alcoholics Anonymous convention. We do not offer people what they really need."[7]

Second, and perhaps even more problematic, was the irreconcilable dissonance between seeker sensitivity, as commonly contextualized in the 1990s, and the Bible's view of spiritual growth.

An indispensable point of departure for a biblical doctrine of sanctification is the notion that God is more concerned about changing our character than changing our circumstances. God's primary goal in my life is to conform me into the image of Christ—not to make my relationships or my job more satisfying and thereby to improve my quality of life.

The most significant growth in the Christian life often occurs as we faithfully persevere through adverse circumstances: "suffering produces endurance, and endurance produces character, and character produces hope" (Rom 5:3–4). To know Christ most intimately, Paul reminds us, is "to know the power of his resurrection in the sharing of his sufferings by becoming like him in his death" (Phil 3:10, my translation). Get this wrong and any attempt to craft a genuinely Christian theology of spiritual formation goes completely off the rails.

Anyone who has stayed the course during a particularly challenging season of life will readily attest to the fact that God uses tough circumstances to grow us up. Indeed, we generally experience more growth when things fail to go our way. As Mike Lueken has recently observed, "There is hardly a better catalyst for transformation than to *not* get what we want."[8] The inevitable dry seasons of a lifelong marriage are a prime example. So are health challenges, vocational disappointments, and financial crises.

---

7. Carlson and Lueken, *Renovation of the Church*, 35, 68 (italics added). Sadly, some church growth literature explicitly encourages us to embrace consumerism as "a fact of life," and to use it to grow large congregations (Schaller, *Very Large Church*, 100).

8. Carlson and Leuken, *Renovation of the Church*, 116 (italics added).

Remaining faithful during life's trials, however, demands a proper understanding of God's overarching purpose in our lives. Walking with Jesus through the dark valleys of pain and suffering requires a theology of spiritual formation that privileges character over circumstances and that understands that God uses life's many difficulties to conform us into the image of his Son.

If I am informed Sunday after Sunday that God's primary design for me is a "wonderful plan" centered on material and relational fulfillment on this side of eternity, I am not likely to embrace adversity with the kind of hope and tenacity reflected in the passages from Paul's letters cited above. Instead, I may very well become disillusioned when God fails to come through on promises he has never made in the first place.

I do not question the motives of those who championed the cause of seeker sensitivity. The desire of these church leaders to reach their generation for Christ is to be commended. We ought to be sensitive to the needs of a hurting world. The lesson to be learned here has to do with the power of culture to hijack even the best of motives and to seriously compromise the well-intentioned efforts of some of our brightest pastors.

The movement's leaders now generally find themselves in agreement with much of the above analysis. Flagship ministries have engaged in a good bit of course correction after discovering a general lack of spiritual maturity among congregants in seeker-sensitive churches.[9]

Now the challenge is to resocialize a whole generation of Christians to embrace a biblical model of sanctification, a task that would have been much less formidable had we: (a) exercised a bit of cultural awareness, and (b) been as theologically sensitive as we were seeker sensitive, during the early years of the movement.

Attentive to the Spirit of God—
The Spiritual Formation Movement (2000s)

Talbot School of Theology houses a top-rate Institute for Spiritual Formation (ISF). The Institute's Master of Arts in Spiritual Formation & Soul Care has become one of our most popular graduate degree programs. The spiritual formation movement has blossomed through the evangelical church as

---

9. Carlson and Leuken, *Renovation of the Church*, is the story of one such congregation. See, also, Hawkins and Parkinson, *Reveal: Where Are You?*

a welcome response to the lack of attention upon Christian maturation that characterized the seeker-sensitive movement of the 1990s.

The benefits at the level of theological reflection have been significant. Talbot's ISF faculty, under the leadership of Dr. John Coe, has crafted a robust, biblical theology of spirituality and sanctification that provides our students with a rich and lasting foundation for pastoral ministry and for thriving in their own spiritual lives.

Practical expressions of spiritual formation strike me as more of a mixed bag where once again our culture's narrative of personal self-discovery threatens to compromise the more holistic, communal view of spiritual life and growth we encounter in Scripture.

On the positive side, who would not welcome the emphasis upon traditional disciplines such prayer, silence, solitude, simplicity, and so forth—historically proven Christian practices that proponents of the movement have essentially rediscovered for the evangelical church in the West in recent decades?[10]

I also applaud spiritual formation's insistence upon prioritizing the developmental aspects of Christian growth. Our program at Talbot, for example, helps our students to come to grips with issues related to their family upbringing in order to equip them to address challenges they will face as Christian leaders in view of their individual relational biographies.

My concerns about spiritual formation relate primarily to the movement's potential to distance itself from the church and its mission. The practice of spiritual direction is a case in point.

Spiritual Direction as a Parachurch Phenomenon

In the words of Angela Reed, a spiritual director is one who helps others "to notice God's presence and activity in their lives."[11] This, of course, is highly commendable. As Douglas Steere has written in an oft-cited

---

10. See Armstrong, "Rise, Frustration, and Revival," for an overview of the rediscovery of historic Christian practices among evangelicals. Seminal treatments include Foster, *Celebration of Discipline*; and Willard, *Spirit of the Disciplines*. See also Whitney, *Spiritual Disciplines within the Church*.

11. Reed, *Quest for Spiritual Community*, 8–9. Anderson and Reese have assembled from the literature ten mutually informing definitions of spiritual mentoring in an appendix to their book *Spiritual Mentoring*, 174–77. They suggest that a mentor should help those who are mentored to explore three primary themes: (1) Who is God? (2) Who am I? (3) What am I to do with my life? (29, 31).

assertion, "To 'listen' another's soul into a condition of disclosure and discovery may be almost the greatest service that any human being ever performs for another."[12]

In her thoughtful treatment of the practice of spiritual guidance and its relationship to the local church, however, Reed provocatively considers the possibility that "we are interested in spiritual guidance today because it feeds the need we are trained in from birth to give greatest attention to what helps *me* live a fulfilling life—the essence of contemporary spirituality." She elaborates:

> According to this argument, increasing attention to interiority actually harms the church. Spiritual guidance practices may inadvertently reinforce Christian faith and practice that focuses on self rather than communal formation, interiority rather than an outward missional focus, and a de-traditionalized eclecticism rather than a firm theological grounding.[13]

Interestingly enough, some spiritual formation programs affirm a parachurch context for spiritual guidance. Graduates set up shop as professional spiritual directors for any and all who might take advantage of their skills and training—apart from any mutual connection with a faith community and its mission.

This is unfortunate. Normalizing spiritual direction as a parachurch ministry strikes me as highly problematic both for our churches and for the spiritual formation movement. The idea of paying someone who is not a part of my local church community for spiritual direction flies in the face of New Testament ecclesiology.

To be fair, we have all benefited from the input of persons outside our faith community. Perhaps it was a book you read or a friend who attends another church. Maybe it was a Christian therapist you saw for a few months. The spiritual resources of the universal church often serve as

---

12. Steere, *Gleanings*, 86.

13. Reed, *Quest for Spiritual Community*, 9–10.

Copan's exegetical analysis of Paul as a spiritual director (*Saint Paul as Spiritual Director*) has much to offer here. In an article summarizing the book's findings, Copan notes that Paul "does not have inner harmony, and mystical experiences, and a sense of oneness with God as the ultimate goal" of spiritual direction. This contrasts sharply with much that is going on in modern spiritual direction, which Copan describes as "a subtle form of spiritual narcissism that speaks of God, yet does not have as its aim the development of a cruciform life." (Copan, "Spiritual Formation and St. Paul as Spiritual Director," 153).

a helpful complement to our pilgrimage among our own church family. Might this be the case for the practice of spiritual direction, as well?

Given the attitude of many congregational leaders toward the spiritual formation movement, moreover, the parachurch setting is hardly surprising. Certain conservative expressions of American evangelicalism tend to view spiritual formation with a great deal of suspicion. Churches belonging to such traditions are generally unwilling to make room in their communities for the practice of spiritual direction. Practitioners are forced to adopt a parachurch approach.

This trend remains regrettable, for spiritual direction belongs in the local church. Isolating the practice from community and mission opens the door to an unhealthy preoccupation with one's personal spiritual pilgrimage. It then becomes easy to lose sight of the more pressing and biblical consideration of our place among the people of God and engaging in the mission of God. In this regard, Reed asks, "Do spiritual guidance practices contribute to the formation of *person, community,* and *mission* or do they emphasize one of these three at the expense of the others?"[14]

Spiritual Direction Belongs in the Local Church

Those training others to do spiritual direction could learn much from Reed's work. What distinguishes her approach is Reed's insistence (a) that "the journey of spiritual formation requires a community characterized by nurture and accountability" and (b) that spiritual direction should be situated in the local church:

> The congregation is called by God to provide exactly what the model of practice includes: relationships that incorporate inward and outward awareness of God, nurture and accountability, along with discernment of calling and opportunities for service.[15]

After all, who should know us better than the members of our own church family?

In my own case, who is better equipped to give me spiritual guidance than my brothers on the elder board, men with whom I have prayed nearly

---

14. Reed, *Quest for Spiritual Community*, 10 (italics original).

15. Ibid., 158. Reed's approach contrasts sharply with that of Anderson and Reese, for example, whose otherwise helpful treatment of the dynamics of spiritual direction (*Spiritual Mentoring*) fails to consider the relationship between the practice and local church ministry.

every Tuesday for more than twenty years? Someone outside my church who has had formal training in spiritual direction?

I think not. The parachurch spiritual director is at a distinct disadvantage because unlike my fellow elders, he cannot observe me interacting with others in the primary relational context God has provided for my growth in Christ. Nor can he watch me use my gifts to serve the mission of the church. This, I suggest, seriously compromises such a director's ability to assist me with (among other things) "discernment of calling and opportunities for service," as Reed expressed it above.

As Reed rightly observes, the reason spiritual guidance has in many cases become a parachurch phenomenon is that the church is not the community God intends it to be. When we begin to enjoy genuine surrogate sibling relationships with our brothers and sisters in Christ, spiritual direction will be the natural fruit of a healthy local church family. It certainly was for me, at any rate.

It was 1977. I had been a Christian for two years. The initial exhilaration and enthusiasm of my newfound faith had worn off a bit, and I had yet to find my place in the dynamics of church life and ministry. Paul Isensee, our minister of music, noticed my aimlessness and asked to "disciple" me (our term back then for giving spiritual guidance). He wanted us to meet weekly one-on-one. But he also wanted to help me find a place of service in the church (a.k.a. "mission"). So he had me organize and lead a youth choir.

Paul and I met together for the better part of a year. We prayed together. We studied the life of Jesus in the Gospels. And we spent a lot of time planning choir tours and debriefing my experience as a choir director. In retrospect, the year together with Paul proved to be one of my most important periods of self-discovery in over forty years as a Christian.

For one thing, I discovered that I was a lousy musical conductor. So I passed the baton (literally) to another fellow in the young adult group. But I also discovered that I loved working with young people and that they responded to my leadership. The youth choir became a springboard to youth ministry, and my wife and I have been pouring ourselves into the lives of others ever since.

Paul, more than anyone else at the time, helped me "to notice God's presence and activity" in my life. Without any training in spiritual guidance, Paul was adequately equipped as a brother in Christ to "listen" my soul "into a condition of disclosure and discovery," as Steele expresses it.

We can debate the need to formally train people to be spiritual directors. It was not necessary in Paul Isensee's case, but it may prove helpful for other leaders who are less intuitively relational in temperament.

The point here has to do with the context in which Paul ministered. As Reed accurately notes,

> Spiritual guidance is founded on the theological perspective that growth in faith is not just individual, it is wholly communal . . . More than anything else, it is the experience of loving human community that makes spiritual guidance a fruitful ministry.[16]

The spiritual direction I received from Paul was a natural expression of a healthy church family. It was deeply rooted, moreover, in the mission of the local church.

This is crucial. Spiritual direction involves more than helping another Christian to cultivate an inward awareness of the presence of God in his or her life. As Reed asserts, "Genuine spiritual formation and spiritual guidance necessarily lead outward" to the discovery of one's gifts, one's calling, and one's role in the mission of the church.[17]

As Paul Isensee wisely recognized, this kind of discernment happens best when our brothers and sisters notice and affirm our character, our gifts, and our abilities in the context of local church life and ministry—that is, when the members of the *body* of Christ become the *voice* of Christ in our lives. Precisely because the guidance I received from Paul was church based and mission oriented, it contributed in a balanced way to Reed's "formation of *person, community,* and *mission*" in ways an individualistic, parachurch approach to the discipline will rarely do.

There is much to commend in the spiritual formation movement, to the degree that the movement directly serves the mission of the local church. Serious theological reflection on the dynamics of spirituality, along with the proper appropriation of traditional spiritual disciplines, can only strengthen the people of God for the mission of God.

Preoccupation with individual spiritual formation divorced from the context of community and mission, however, is a dead-end street. We grow in Christ to the degree that we are relationally grounded in a healthy Christian community that is sold out to the ministry of the gospel.[18]

16. Ibid., 137.
17. Ibid., 96.
18. For a more thorough evaluation of the spiritual formation movement, including both appropriate affirmation and insightful critique, see Langer, "Points of Unease."

Some Important Qualifications

The above analysis sharply emphasized the downside of several recent trends among American evangelicals. The strident tone was intentional and necessary in order to make a point. But it was also a bit unfair, since in each case there has been a significant upside, as well.

God used *The Four Spiritual Laws*, for example, to bring multitudes to Christ. Interestingly enough, moreover, many of us who utilized this evangelistic tool had a higher ecclesiology than the tract itself. Well aware of the crucial role that Christian community played in our own spiritual lives, we did what we could to make sure that family and friends who responded positively to *The Four Spiritual Laws* found their way into a local church.

The spiritual gifts craze of the 1980s was also fruitful, in spite of the misdirected focus on self-discovery. Preoccupation with discovering our gifts mobilized many of God's people for ministry. Thoughtful pastors who encouraged church members to find their gifts often balanced the culture's focus on personal fulfillment with the Bible's emphasis on the edification of the body.

Neither was the seeker-sensitive movement wholly without value. Attention to the rapidly changing needs and preferences of unbelievers in the shifting cultural landscape of late twentieth-century America generated a healthy course correction in some areas of ministry. (Music comes most immediately to mind.) It was also the case that larger seeker-sensitive churches, which had the necessary resources, sought to complement the "God-wants-to-meet-your-needs" mentality on Sunday mornings with a "digging deeper" service on Wednesday nights and small-group offerings throughout the week.

The spiritual formation movement may bear even more fruit. Two aspects of the movement positively distinguish it from the earlier trends discussed above. First, most of the cutting-edge work in spiritual formation is being done among thoughtful, self-critical academics who, in my experience, seem less likely than local church leaders to be taken captive by the consumerism and radical individualism of our surrounding culture.

Second, much of what is called spiritual formation today is not new at all, since the movement's roots and practices reach far back into the rich, time-tested history of the Christian church. These characteristics bode well for the future of spiritual formation and its potential to contribute much to the health and the mission of the local church.

We will never completely get it right as Christian leaders. In our efforts to reach culture, we will inevitably be taken captive by culture, to some degree at any rate. Fortunately, God in his boundless grace and mercy will continue to use our flawed ideas and programs to do his kingdom work. He always has.

Nevertheless, the view of Christian spirituality exhibited in the trends examined above clearly represents a marked and regrettable departure from the community-centered mindset of biblical Christianity that we encountered in the first chapters of this book. The troubling disconnect between (a) the communal priorities of New Testament Christianity and (b) the me-orientation of modern evangelicalism has justified a good degree of historical reflection and pointed cultural critique.

Conclusion

It is not hard to see how (1) the anthropocentric approach to evangelism found in gospel tracts like *The Four Spiritual Laws*, (2) the framing of spiritual gifts in terms of personal fulfillment, and (3) the felt-needs focus of the seeker-sensitive movement contributed significantly to the seismic shift from "us" to "me" that occurred during the latter half of the twentieth century among American evangelicals.

We should hardly be surprised to discover with Barna that, by 1998, American Christians viewed our faith as "a commodity that we consume, rather than one in which we invest ourselves." After all, we had just spent the better part of three decades socializing ourselves to view our relationship with God and his church in precisely these terms.

6

Enjoying the Presence of God

Spiritual Formation and the Quest for Religious Experience

> People are meant to live in an ongoing conversation with God, speaking and being spoken to.
>
> —Dallas Willard[1]

I spent my first decade as a Christian in a church that viewed learning about God and serving God as more central to the faith than experiencing God's presence in our personal lives or in our weekly gatherings as a community.

We did give a good deal of attention to the topic of prayer. And our new-believers curriculum included a chapter titled "How to Walk in the Spirit." There was also a great deal of emphasis on having a "personal relationship with God."

Most of us did not expect that relationship to cash out, however, in a subjective, moment-by-moment awareness of the Holy Spirit's presence or leading in our lives. Indeed, some very popular tracts and books explicitly warned against preoccupation with religious experience in the Christian life.

The Four Spiritual Laws, for example, devoted a whole page to a section titled "Do Not Depend on Feelings." Many readers will recall the familiar train diagram:

---

1. Willard, *Hearing God*, 20.

The accompanying text explains:

> The train will run with or without the caboose. However, it would be useless to attempt to pull the train by the caboose. In the same way, as Christians we do not depend on feelings or emotions, but we place our faith (trust) in the trustworthiness of God and the promises of His Word.[2]

My early experiences in vocational Christian ministry only served to reinforce the above priorities.

A Message from God

During the early 1980s, I was pastor of single adults in a large evangelical church. Most of our singles desired to be married. For one young man this longing created more than a little theological and relational chaos in our singles group.

One Sunday Alex informed me that he was going to marry Jennifer, a young woman in the group. I found this rather intriguing, because I knew that the two of them were not dating at the time. I probed a bit and discovered that God had told Alex that Jennifer was going to be his wife.

I initially tried to restrain myself from asking the obvious question. Then I gave in and inquired, "Has God told Jennifer about this, Alex?"

God had not told Jennifer. But this did not seem to be a problem for Alex. He had a divine revelation, a message from God that was confirmed in his mind the following Sunday when he put God to the test: "If Jennifer sits down in front of me in church this Sunday, I will know that she is the one."

---

2. Bright, *Four Spiritual Laws*, 12.

Remarkably enough, Jennifer found a spot in the pew directly in front of Alex that morning—right where she always sat in church on Sunday. It was not long before I had to have a "Back off, buddy!" chat with Alex.

I also did my best to address the relational hurt that Alex's experience with God caused Jennifer. To her credit, Jennifer was determined to remain in community with her church family, in spite of the sanctified stalking she had experienced with Alex.

The debacle with Alex and Jennifer was not an isolated event. I soon found out that another fellow in the group had received a similar "message from God."

I clearly needed to help our singles craft a biblical theology of God's will and to understand the role of the Spirit's guidance when seeking a mate. Fortunately, I stumbled across just the resource I needed to teach on the topic.

Garry Freisen had recently released the first (1980) edition of *Decision Making and the Will of God: A Biblical Alternative to the Traditional View*.[3] Freisen's basic thesis is that God has no "perfect will" for our lives when it comes to choosing a mate or making any other major decision. Within God's moral will, as revealed in Scripture, we are free to choose as we please, exercising the general wisdom that God has given us.

Thus, a woman whose husband has died is "free to be married to whom she wishes, only in the Lord" (1 Cor 7:39). God does not really care whom the widow marries, as long as the man is a Christian.

Freisen's book was a game changer, and much of the reasoning remains biblical and liberating. The inevitable corollary of such a view, however, for better or for worse, is to relegate religious experience to the back burner of the Christian life.

After all, if we do not need the Holy Spirit to guide us in making major life decisions, what do we need him for? The biblical answers—conviction of sin, assurance of salvation, and so forth—were inadequate at the time to overcome negative attitudes toward religious experience in noncharismatic evangelical churches.

This general hermeneutic of suspicion regarding anything experiential in the Christian life influenced expectations for Sunday gatherings as well. One morning our music director introduced a song that invited the Holy Spirit to come and join us as we worshiped. Several of the church's theological gatekeepers found the song highly problematic.

---

3. Multnomah Publishers released a twenty-fifth-anniversary edition in 2004.

Enjoying the Presence of God

"The Holy Spirit is already here," they asserted. "He came at Pentecost" (Acts 2). The idea the Spirit might manifest himself in some extraordinary, experiential way one Sunday was nowhere on these folks' radar screen except, perhaps, as an enemy bogey that needed to be taken out before it could do any damage to the church.

A Tectonic Shift

Those who protested the song that Sunday would soon find themselves on the losing side of what was to become a heated debate among evangelicals about music and worship. "Come, Holy Spirit" was an early expression of a tectonic shift that would not only change the way we programmed music in our churches but also completely reorient our attitudes about the experiential aspects of the faith.

Virtually all of the music produced in the early years of the transition from traditional to contemporary music (between the mid-1970s until the 1990s) came from neo-Pentecostal, charismatic groups, for whom religious experience was an essential aspect of worship. Vineyard USA, for example, lists as one of the denomination's core values "Experience & Worship God." Accordingly, the Vineyard movement asserts that "the experience of the kingdom of God (and thus, the experience of God's presence) is central to our faith and Christian life."[4]

Our church traded choir and organ for a band and praise songs in the late 1980s. Other traditional, noncharismatic congregations did the same. Music produced in charismatic circles began increasingly to shape our thinking about the nature of God's presence, not only in corporate worship, but in other aspects of the Christian life as well. It was not long before experiencing God began to take center stage in reflection about Christian spirituality among charismatics and noncharismatics alike.

Most influential at the popular level was Henry Blackaby's *Experiencing God: Knowing and Doing the Will of God*. The workbook, which first appeared more than twenty-five years ago, has since sold millions of copies worldwide. The publisher's claim that "the Experiencing God ministry is even more vibrant today than when it began" can hardly be challenged. The original workbook has generated a virtual cottage industry of ancillary publications, including an abbreviated book titled *7 Truths From Experiencing*

---

4. Vineyard USA, "Core Values."

God, student editions of both the workbook and the shorter version, daily devotionals, and an audio devotional CD set.[5]

Noted Christian thinkers began to revisit the topic of God's will and the leading of the Holy Spirit. Philosopher Dallas Willard directly challenged Freisen's paradigm in a widely read book designed to provide "*a clear understanding* and *a confident, practical orientation toward God's way of guiding us and communicating with us.*"[6] For Willard, hearing from God is a given: "As Christians we stand in a millennia-long tradition of humans who have been addressed by God."[7]

Watershed treatments of Christian spirituality by those on the forefront of the spiritual formation movement now routinely address religious experience, some in great detail. Thus, Evan Howard devotes a chapter each to "Human Experience" and "Christian Experience" in his fine textbook, *Introduction to Christian Spirituality*.[8] A three-chapter section in Kenneth Boa's *Conformed to His Image* "stresses the biblical implications of the Holy Spirit as a personal presence."[9]

We should not be surprised to see theologians in the spiritual formation movement grappling conceptually with the phenomenon of religious experience. Numbers of practices promoted by the movement assume as normative the experiential presence of God in our lives. Spiritual direction is a case in point, since a spiritual director is one who helps others "to notice God's presence and activity in their lives."[10]

How are we to evaluate this tectonic shift in thinking about the role and value of religious experience in the Christian life? Is current enthusiasm about experiencing God beneficial? Is it biblical?

One can hardly argue with what appears to be a return to a more holistic view of the spiritual life, provided it is genuinely holistic, with experience taking its appropriate place alongside other essentials of the Christian life (e.g., the Bible, community, and outreach). I will adopt a cautiously optimistic approach to religious experience when I consider in some detail what it means to experience God later in the chapter.

---

5. Blackaby, *Experiencing God*. See also http://www.lifeway.com/ for other products.s
6. Willard, *Hearing God*, 31 (italics original).
7. Ibid., 24.
8. Howard, *Brazos Introduction to Christian Spirituality*, 77–112, 145–94.
9. Boa, *Conformed to His Image*, 289–321. The quote is from a summary on p. 15.
10. Reed, *Quest for Spiritual Community*, 8–9.

Enjoying the Presence of God

First, however, a bit of cultural analysis is in order. As we saw in chapter 5, significant shifts in Christian theology and practice seldom happen in isolation from broader cultural currents in the secular arena. As we reflect upon the place of religious experience in the Christian life, it is important to recognize that we inhabit a culture that has become obsessed with the quest for experience in nearly every area of life.

When Life Lacks Meaning

Many of us in Western society find ourselves in a day-to-day routine that lacks the sense of existential significance for which God has designed us. We are bored. So we substitute experiences of various kinds to remind us that we are alive.

Roland Rolheiser accurately describes the mindset of many in postmodern America today:

> Our lives become consumed with the idea that unless we somehow experience everything, travel everywhere, see everything, and are part of a large number of other people's experience, then our own lives are small and meaningless.[11]

Some of these experiences are enriching. Others are less so. Taken together they tell us something about the sense of dissatisfaction many of us have with our daily lives.

Consider travel, for instance. The great majority of people in history past never traveled far from their place of birth.

My parents did not own a car. They walked to work. The Hellermans never went on vacation to another state, let alone another country. Mom and Dad did not feel the need to experience a different culture or a different place. They were content to stay put.

Today no one stays put. We assume we are missing out on something important in life if we do not experience new places and different cultures.

Last night I visited a young man in our church family who is battling cancer. I read Scripture and prayed for him. Then, to cheer him up a bit, I asked him, "Ron, let's say you beat this thing and start life fresh and healthy a couple months from now. What do you want to do with your life?"

Ron's response: "I want to travel to Asia, to New Zealand, and to Europe."

---

11. Rolheiser, *Shattered Lantern*, 37.

There is certainly something to be said for broadening our geographical and cultural horizons. Exposure to other cultures brings a welcome challenge to the unbiblical ethnocentrism that generally marks the lives of persons raised in a monocultural setting. For those who have the luxury to afford it, travel can be an enlightening and enriching experience. In another sense, however, our wanderlust functions as just one of many avenues of escape from the meaningless routine of our daily lives.

Travel is not all we do to break the routine. We go out to eat. We go to the movies. We go to a concert. We attend a major sporting event.

Greeks and Romans had their theaters, amphitheaters, and stadiums. A few writers, including Herodotus (c. 440 BCE), even penned travelogues for fellow elites who had the time and luxury to read them. People have always enjoyed an occasional escape from normalcy.

But not to the degree that we do today.

When I was growing up, my family seldom went out to dinner or the movies. We never went to a concert. Dad did take me to see the Los Angeles Dodgers one time.

I remain highly intrigued by the fact that my parents apparently did not feel compelled to experience a lot of the things that I and my adult children seem to need to experience. They found sufficient meaning in what we view as the mundane routine of daily life.

Why am I so different from my parents? Why were my parents so apparently content with the repetitive rhythms of daily living? A big part of the answer, I think, is quite obvious. My parents did not grow up with television or any other visual electronic media, for that matter. Today, media, driven by a multimillion-dollar advertising machine, is ubiquitous. And our consumer culture has a single overarching goal that it depends on for its very existence. That goal is to convince you and me that we are not okay—that we are not really living—unless we drive the right car, eat the latest food, wear the most fashionable clothes, and visit the most exotic places.

I receive a monthly e-mail informing me of the hottest new restaurants in Hermosa Beach, California. The implicit message is that I will remain hopelessly impoverished as a human being if I fail to experience the latest in local cuisine.

The sophistication of the consumer enterprise has become astounding. Several days ago I made the mistake of searching the Internet to get the specs on the most recent version of the stage piano that I play with my

Enjoying the Presence of God

blues band. You know what is coming next. The following day I found myself inundated with targeted advertising for electronic keyboards; the ads were plastered all over my Facebook page. The message? Joe Hellerman will never be the best musician he can be unless he pulls the trigger on that new three-thousand-dollar Nord 3 stage piano.

The point here is that our media culture has effectively socialized us to feel that we are incomplete, empty—even meaningless, if we do not experience the latest and greatest in every area of our lives. Little wonder we are dissatisfied with the routine of our day-to-day existence.

Things were completely different for my parents. Because they were raised in the first half of the twentieth century, Mom and Dad "missed out" on the media revolution. With no one to constantly remind them what they were lacking, my parents felt content with what they had—and with what they did—day in and day out.

So it was for most people of my parents' generation. And this has been the norm for the great majority of human beings throughout world history. Indeed, when we gain a little perspective, we surprisingly discover that our incessant quest for repeated experiential escape from the daily grind is a historical and cultural anomaly.

Consider another anomaly. Major League baseball pitcher Zach Greinke earns approximately eleven thousand dollars every time he tosses a baseball a little over sixty feet. And this estimate is surely on the low side, since it assumes that Greinke, who in 2015 signed a six-year, $206,500,000 contract with the Arizona Diamondbacks, will throw one hundred pitches in thirty games this year, a highly unlikely scenario.

Actually, the Diamondbacks do not pay Greinke to pitch for them. We do. And this says volumes about the priority we place on entertainment. The people we value and reward are not those who make us better human beings—teachers, social workers, counselors, ministers. The people we value are the ones who most effectively entertain us by providing a diversion from the routines of our daily lives.

My intention here is not to make a value judgment about these activities. My wife and I like to travel. I wrote much of this book while on vacation in the mountains during a summer break from the university. And one of my co-pastors happens to be the chaplain for the Los Angeles Dodgers. We can debate the relative value for human flourishing of the activities discussed above.

Our dissatisfaction with the daily routine generates other behaviors, however, that are clearly unhealthy. A fellow I met on a fishing trip told me that he has three homes: one each in California, Arkansas, and Florida. He gets bored living in one place.

I told him, "I'm not bored and I've lived in the same house for more than sixty years."

His reply was highly revealing: "I can't live in the same place. And I can't have sex with the same woman."

Millions of Americans escape the meaningless monotony of life by turning to drugs, alcohol, pornography, or gambling. Others rely on the more socially acceptable mechanisms of extreme sports such as bungee jumping or cliff diving. We live from one dopamine rush to the next.

Scientists still do not understand all the clever things that dopamine does. We do know, however, that: (1) dopamine is a chemical "released in our brains in response to rewarding experiences"; and (2) dopamine "makes us want to do whatever we can to get more of those experiences."[12]

Don't miss the word *experiences* in both quotations. Fleeting experience has become the unfortunate substitute for purpose and meaning in the lives of many in postmodern America. Could this be the case for our spiritual lives as well?

Experiencing God

Books and discipleship curricula purporting to help us experience God sell millions of copies. Pentecostal and charismatic movements of various stripes center on engaging with God in subjective, experiential ways. Believers move from church to church seeking a more stimulating worship experience or more dynamic teaching.

Can we really put experiencing God in the same category as the above activities? Could my desire to subjectively experience the presence of God be merely another attempt to escape from a boring daily routine, a quest that reveals how little meaning I find in life?

Yes and no.

In the Bible we see the people of God experiencing their Lord in some remarkable and powerful ways. God wants us to experience his presence, in our churches and in our individual lives. Our spirits and our emotions are

---

12. Carnell, "Bad Boys, Bad Brains."

Enjoying the Presence of God

closely connected. To not have the "joy of the Lord," for example, is to not have much of the Lord at all.

I suspect, moreover, that for the apostle Paul joy was far more than simply a cognitive mindset about the character of God that gave him the resources to buck up in the face of adverse circumstances. It was a deeply immediate experience of the presence and purpose of God in his life.[13]

Union with Christ should not remain merely a propositional bullet point in a theological treatise on soteriology. It should cash out in an existential experience of the presence of God in our lives. It certainly did for the apostle Paul, and he longed for the same in the lives of his converts.[14]

Clarification is in order, however, when we talk about religious experience. Just how does the Holy Spirit manifest God's presence to us? Should we actively pursue the felt presence of God in our walk with Christ?

What It Means to Experience God

In the New Testament the Holy Spirit appears to manifest God's immediate presence to us in two fundamental ways:

1. Ordinary manifestations of the indwelling Spirit. (John 14:16–17, 23; Rom 8:9–17)

2. Extraordinary manifestations of the Spirit's power and other ecstatic experiences of God (Acts 4:31; 13:9; 2 Cor 12:1–4)

Both 1 and 2 involve an affective component and can thus be understood in relation to the existential experience of God in our lives. But they show some important differences, as well.

Let us consider first the ongoing activity of God's Spirit in our lives (#1).[15] Jesus promised his disciples,

---

13. Scholars have become increasingly sensitive to the role that emotions play in our spiritual lives. Chandler devotes a chapter to the topic, for example, in *Christian Spiritual Formation*, 83–105. Note also Issler, "Soul and Spiritual Formation," 128–36.

14. New Testament texts often cited to support this notion include John 14:23; Rom 5:5, 8:16; Eph 3:16; Phil 4:13; Col 1:29; and 2 Tim 4:17. Porter helpfully responds to concerns that the spiritual formation movement is "overly experiential" in "Sanctification in a New Key." For a thoughtful treatment of the experiential nature of our union with Christ, see Davis, *Meditation and Communion with God*, 41–51.

15. I am following Porter, "Sanctification in a New Key," and the works he cites. I am also indebted to Porter for his feedback on an earlier draft of the chapter. He has helped me to think much more clearly about what it means to experience God.

> "I will ask the Father, and he will give you another Helper, to be with you forever, even the Spirit of truth . . . I will not leave you as orphans." (John 14:16–18)
>
> Judas (not Iscariot) said to him, "Lord, how is it that you will manifest yourself to us, and not to the world?" Jesus answered him, "If anyone loves me, he will keep my word, and my Father will love him, and we will come to him and make our home with him." (John 14:22–23)

It would be counterintuitive to exclude an experiential component from the dynamic that Jesus describes here in John 14. As D. A. Carson notes, "The Spirit is to be experienced; otherwise the promise . . . of relief from the sense of abandonment is empty."[16]

It is a profitable exercise to consider just how the indwelling Spirit manifests the Father and Son to the believer (cf. vv. 22–23, above). We may assume that conviction of sin and encouragement toward obedience are in the mix, as well as the subjective assurance that we are children of God (Rom 8:15–16).

More is involved as well. J. I. Packer, for example, speaks of the Spirit granting "perceptions of [God's] greatness and goodness, his eternity and infinity, his truth, his love, and his glory."[17]

This is clearly the case with respect to our apprehension of God's love in Christ. According to Paul, it is the ministry of "the Spirit" in our "inner being" that enables us to "comprehend with all the saints what is the breadth and length and height and depth, and to know the love of Christ that surpasses knowledge" (Eph 3:16–19; see chapter 1 for a communal understanding of this dynamic).

For all these reasons, scholars such as Steve Porter emphasize "the fundamental truth that life in the Spirit has an experiential dimension."[18]

The (1) ordinary presence of God's Spirit in our lives is to be distinguished, however, from (2) extraordinary manifestations of the Spirit's power and other ecstatic experiences of God.

First of all, our conscious awareness of the Spirit's ordinary presence waxes and wanes. Thus, although Scripture assures us that God never

---

16. Carson, *The Gospel according to John*, 500.
17. Packer, *Keeping in Step with The Spirit*, 62.
18. Porter, "Sanctification in a New Key," 145.

Enjoying the Presence of God

abandons us, we read in Christian literature about a dark night of the soul, when we are hardly aware of God's presence at all in an experiential sense.[19]

Many of us have been there. When this occurs, it is comforting to know, as Thomas Merton asserts, that "[God] may be more present to us when He is absent than when He is present."[20] The point is that we are not always consciously aware of the ordinary manifestations of the indwelling Spirit.

Consider, by way of example, our assurance of salvation. In Rom 8:16, Paul informs us that the Spirit "bears witness to our spirit that we are children of God."[21] The context makes it clear that Paul is speaking of the ordinary manifestation of the indwelling Spirit in the life of a believer, so we can be confident that the Spirit's testimony here is constant. Our felt-experience of this filial relationship varies in intensity, however, during the course our Christian lives.

Just the opposite is the case for extraordinary manifestations of the Spirit. These are invariably a part of our conscious awareness. Indeed, they generally dominate our conscious awareness when they occur. It is the dramatic nature of these experiences that makes them extraordinary.

A second distinction relates to the place of the two phenomena in Christian life and practice. I will argue below that, among the early Christians, religious experience in the sense of #2 above was a by-product of community and mission, generally directed toward the accomplishment of some special purpose of God.

The ordinary work of the Spirit in our lives is much more foundational. By way of example, our apprehension of God's constant love—enabled, according to Paul, by the ongoing presence of the Spirit in our lives (Eph 3:16–19)—is no by-product but is rather the basis and motivation for everything we do as Christians: "We love because he first loved us" (John 4:19).

---

19. The discussion extends back into late antiquity. See recently Coe, "Musings." Coe focuses on developmental spirituality as articulated by Saint John of the Cross.

20. Merton, *No Man Is an Island*, 250.

21. The Greek term translated "(our) spirit" is to be read as an indirect object ("to"), and not a dative of association ("with"), per Wallace *Greek Grammar*, 159. Wallace, "Witness of the Spirit," elaborates by asserting that the inner witness of the Spirit "involves a non-discursive presence that is recognized in the soul." The beautiful irony of this post is that Wallace here marshals his prodigious skills as a scholar to mount a detailed, cognitive argument for what he labels the "supra-logical" witness of the Spirit, which, in the final analysis, is "not verifiable on an empirical plane."

This brings us to a third and final difference. We can train ourselves—and train one another—to become increasingly sensitive to the ordinary ministry of the Holy Spirit even as the felt presence of God waxes and wanes in our lives. Extraordinary manifestations of the Spirit are, in contrast, dependent upon the sovereignty of God, who does what he pleases, when he pleases, to further the expansion of the gospel.

Longing for God's Special Presence

We are now prepared to return to the question raised above. *Is my desire to subjectively experience the presence of God merely another attempt to escape from a boring daily routine, a quest that reveals how little meaning I find in life?*

If we are talking about experiencing God in the sense described in #1, above, the answer is clearly no. God wants us to sense and respond to the ongoing presence of his Spirit in our lives. This has been a key focus of the spiritual formation movement, and for that we should be grateful.

It is reasonable to assert, however, that our zeal to experience God's presence in extraordinary, non-routine ways (#2)—expressed, for example, in the quest for the most inspiring worship encounter or the most "anointed" Bible teacher—has much in common with the various pursuits of experiential escape that characterize the rest of our lives in the postmodern West.

The parallel is actually striking. Bored with the daily routine of school, work, dishes, laundry, and so forth, we seek out experiences of various sorts to inject a sense of meaning into our lives. Dissatisfied with the ordinary presence of God's abiding Spirit in our lives, we long for God to show up in extraordinary ways.

Extraordinary religious experience offers an easy and potentially exhilarating alternative to the routine ministry of the Holy Spirit in our lives. Steve Porter, a colleague at Talbot School of Theology, recently suggested that one reason we prefer extraordinary—over ordinary—experiences with God is that the ordinary manifestation of the Spirit challenges us to die to self. Extraordinary experiences with the Spirit are not nearly as demanding and confrontational at the core of our being.

A woman in my church recently articulated this very distinction. She asked me, "Joe, when we sing 'Come Holy Spirit,' are we asking to feel God's presence in some special way? Or are we asking the Spirit to come and convict us of sin?" I had to come to grips with the reality that I generally sing the refrain hoping for some extraordinary manifestation of the Spirit that will make me feel good about God, giving little thought to the Holy Spirit's ministry of conviction of sin.

Our longing to feel the special presence of God may tell us something about where we are at as evangelicals in our spiritual pilgrimage, both as individuals and as a movement. Christian thinkers past and present who have reflected on the phenomenon, view the felt need for subjective religious experience as characteristic of the earliest stage of spiritual growth. John Coe summarizes the teachings of Saint John of the Cross: "God provides spiritual infants with pleasure regarding spiritual things in accordance with their pre-converted appetite for pleasure in finite objects."[22] God in his mercy meets our need for spiritual pleasure as infants. Later he at times withdraws his felt presence, in order to grow us up. The goal is to move us beyond the love of God for (spiritual) pleasure's sake to a love of God for God's sake.[23]

God's Special Presence and God's Priorities

The point of all this is to help us to come to grips with a fundamental biblical truth. Among the early Christians, extraordinary religious experience was not a goal to be sought by the individual believer in the course of his or her private spiritual pilgrimage.

The apostle Paul is a case in point. Paul treasured his relationship with Jesus. But we do not see Paul focusing upon subjective religious experience the way many of us do today. Neither does he encourage his converts to do so. In fact, Paul will only relate his most extraordinary experience of God—he was "caught up to the third heaven" and "heard things that cannot be told" (2 Cor 12:2–4)—when he is forced to engage in a little foolish "boasting" (vv. 1, 12) to spar with his Corinthian opponents, who, unlike Paul, seem to have put ecstatic experience at the center of their Christian faith.

Most important, in the New Testament era, experiencing God's extraordinary presence was almost exclusively connected to engaging in God's mission, and to doing so in community with others, topics to be addressed in detail in the next chapter.

---

22. Coe, "Musings," 296.
23. Ibid., 295.

Why We Need the Church to Become More Like Jesus

I suspect that the early Christians experienced God in the ways they did not because they placed experiencing God at the center of the Christian life. They experienced God so powerfully because they were sold out to God's mission to reach the world together for Jesus, and God at times met them in extraordinary ways to assist them in accomplishing his missional purposes.

God's power and God's presence follow God's priorities. Notice that the promise of Jesus's personal presence is tied directly to the Great Commission in Matt 28:19–20:

> Go therefore and make disciples of all nations, baptizing them in the name of the Father and of the Son and of the Holy Spirit, teaching them to observe all that I have commanded you. And behold, I am with you always, to the end of the age.

Jesus makes the same connection in the first chapter of Acts:

> You will receive power when the Holy Spirit has come upon you, and you will be my witnesses in Jerusalem and in all Judea and Samaria, and to the end of the earth. (1:8)

It is not my intention to set up a false dichotomy between our experience of God on the one hand and the mission of God on the other. Both are clearly biblical. Equally biblical, however, is the relationship we encounter in the Scriptures between non-routine religious experience and the task that God has set before us.

The people in our churches today who experience God in the most intimate and powerful ways are not those who seek after extraordinary manifestations of the Spirit. Rather, they are disciples of Jesus who have given their lives over to God's disciple-making mission. How did Jesus put it? "Whoever would save his life will lose it, but whoever loses his life for my sake and the gospel's will save it" (Mark 8:35).

Conclusion

Much more could be said about the affective dynamics of our relationship with God, but the above observations will have to suffice for now.[24] We turn in the next chapter to the topic of outreach and its role in spiritual formation.

Experiencing God and serving God are not unrelated. God offers a wonderful alternative to an otherwise aimless life that must rely on regular shots of experiential escape—secular or spiritual—to provide a sense of significance. That alternative is to give our lives to a *community* with a *mission*—a local church charged with the task of proclaiming the "excellencies" of the God who has called us "out of darkness into his marvelous light" (1 Pet 2:9).

No one knew better than Simon Peter that God's power and presence follow God's priorities. Peter was "filled with the Spirit" in a special way (Acts 4:8) when he proclaimed Christ before the Jewish leaders in Jerusalem. Peter's church was "filled with the Spirit" when they prayed for boldness in the face of persecution (Acts 4:31). We turn now to Peter's first letter, where Jesus's inspired apostle invites us to give ourselves to the most meaningful task imaginable: bringing the love of Jesus to a broken world and a broken world to Jesus.

---

24. I have left unaddressed the way we experience God, for example, when we exercise the gifts of the Spirit in corporate worship. Whatever we might conclude about this, it is quite clear that Paul viewed the subjective experience of the individual (apparently a passion of some in Corinth) as wholly secondary to the impact of the ministry of the gifts upon the community (1 Cor 12–14).

7

Hands to the Plow Together

Community, Mission, and Spiritual Formation

> Genuine spiritual formation and spiritual
> guidance necessarily lead outward.
>
> —Angela Reed[1]

> Christian spiritual formation is the process of being conformed
> to the image of Christ for the sake of others.
>
> —M. Robert Mulholland Jr.[2]

"Is Lack of Life Meaning Your Depression Trigger?" So reads the title of a blog post on a website called *Lawyers with Depression*. No lawyer joke here. Depression is serious stuff in the legal profession. And it is often related to "a life that feels meaningless."[3]

One of the keys to beating depression is to find meaning and purpose in what we do. The author suggests that a lawyer whose life lacks meaning should get involved in pro bono work for the underprivileged or perhaps volunteer to train or mentor others.

Alternatively, an attorney whose creative side is constrained by the nature of the legal profession might try playing with Legos, crafting

---

1. Reed, *Quest for Spiritual Community*, 96.
2. Mulholland, *Shaped by the Word*, 25.
3. Lukasik, "Is Lack of Life Meaning Your Depression Trigger?"

origami, or working with clay. Even "a pretty scarf or unusual tie could add a big lift to your life."[4]

Recent inquiry into the relationship between emotional health and purposeful living advocates a more robust approach to depression—one that ideally involves a significant spiritual dimension.

An Antidote for Depression

Researchers at Florida Atlantic University studied the relationship between adult attachment styles, spirituality, and depression among individuals undergoing treatment for substance abuse.[5] For the spirituality component they used the Spiritual Well-Being (SWB) Scale, a diagnostic tool developed in the 1980s, which consists of two subscales:

1. Existential Well-Being (EWB) = Feelings of transcendental purpose and meaning
2. Religious Well-Being (RWB) = Feelings of closeness to God

The EWB had the subjects evaluate themselves against statements like, "I don't know who I am, where I came from, or where I am going." The RWB scale included assertions such as, "I have a personally meaningful relationship with God."[6] The study sought to determine which of these two characteristics of our spiritual lives—existential well-being or religious well-being—best protected the respondents against symptoms of depression.

I expected religious well-being to win, hands down. What could possibly be a better antidote to depression than "a personally meaningful relationship with God"?

I was wrong. The answer surprised even the authors of the study: "The existential-purpose and meaning-in-life dimension of spirituality seems to be the most important factor related to depressive symptoms among this sample of individuals."[7] Remarkably, this remained the case even for persons in the study who were relationally challenged due to insecure attachment styles: "Although individuals' current relationships may not be ideal because of attachment issues, if they have adequate levels of existen-

---

4. Ibid.
5. Diaz et al, "Attachment Style."
6. Ibid., 316.
7. Ibid., 321.

tial purpose and meaning in life, they may be protected against clinical levels of depressive symptoms."[8] The study concludes with suggestions for treating bouts of depression that are often associated with substance abuse: "Although our results suggest that practitioners could consider focusing on promoting improved interpersonal relationships for individuals with insecure attachment styles, they may want to place the fostering of purpose and meaning in life as a higher priority for treatment planning."[9]

Findings like these have implications that reach far beyond the walls of the substance abuse treatment center that housed the respondents to this particular study. For "the fostering of purpose and meaning" is a fundamental quality-of-life factor in each of our lives.

In what follows we will first consider how God has provided for our need for meaning in the Great Commission. We will then look at the New Testament pattern of extending God's love to the world in partnership with our fellow believers.

No Higher Calling

Jesus's disciple Simon Peter beautifully articulates the life of meaning and purpose that God intends for his children, as we partner together to do God's work in the world:

> As you come to him, a living stone rejected by men but in the sight of God chosen and precious, you yourselves like living stones are being built up as a spiritual house, to be a holy priesthood, *to offer spiritual sacrifices acceptable to God through Jesus Christ* . . . But you are a chosen race, a royal priesthood, a holy nation, a people for his own possession, *that you may proclaim the excellencies of him who called you out of darkness into his marvelous light.* 10 Once you were not a people, but now you are God's people; once you had not received mercy, but now you have received mercy. (1 Pet 2:4–5, 9–10; italics added)

I have highlighted the twofold task God has set before us. We "offer spiritual sacrifices" to God (v. 5), and we "proclaim the excellencies" of the One who has delivered us "out of darkness into his marvelous light" (v. 9).

---

8. Ibid., 320.
9. Ibid., 321.

The expression "priesthood" (vv. 5, 9) particularly underscores the significance of the mission into which God has invited every believer.[10] When Peter refers to Christians as a priesthood, he deploys a familiar Old Testament image in a radically new way.

For much of Peter's life, the priesthood had been a special subgroup among the people of God. After God delivered Israel from slavery in Egypt, he designated a single tribe, Levi, to mediate between God and the nation of Israel. Within the Levites themselves, God chose Aaron and his sons to serve as priests at the altar of the tabernacle.

The levitical priesthood stood in the gap, so to speak, between God and his people. The priests brought the people to God by means of Israel's offerings and sacrifices. And they brought God to the people by teaching the law (Num 3–4; 18:1–7; Neh 8:2–8; 2 Chr 17:7–9).

Notice what has changed in 1 Peter 2. The imagery remains the same, but it functions quite differently. Peter now identifies all of God's people as "a holy priesthood" (v. 5). There is no clergy. No laity. We are all part of God's priesthood.

We are called "a *royal* priesthood" (v. 9) as well. This would have been a jarring image for any first-century Jew familiar with Israel's history. King and priest were different offices in the Old Testament. During the monarchy God kept them distinct, presumably because of the potential abuse involved when royal power was combined with priestly privilege. Kings such as Uzziah, who crossed this sacred boundary by attempting to function in a priestly capacity, were severely disciplined (2 Chr 26:16–21).

This changed dramatically through the work of Messiah Jesus, who has become both high priest and king. Accordingly, as Jesus's representatives, we are now a "royal priesthood." It is hard to imagine a Jew like Peter choosing a more dignified, meaningful title for his readers.

The lofty title corresponds to the new priesthood's lofty task. For something else has changed in the transition from old covenant to new covenant. The priesthood Peter describes no longer mediates between God and the rest of God's people. We now stand in the gap between God and the rest of humanity.

Old Testament priests brought Israel to God and God to Israel. We bring the world to God and we bring God to the world.[11]

---

10. For a recent exposition of the doctrine of the priesthood of all believers, see the fine treatment by Anizor and Voss, *Representing Christ*.

11. I have overstated the distinction between the covenants in order to make a

No task gives life more meaning than this one. And it is a mission in which every follower of Jesus can participate.

The Ministry of the New Covenant Priesthood

Peter elaborates on our priestly calling as follows. We bring the world to God when we (1) "offer spiritual sacrifices acceptable to God through Jesus Christ" (v. 5). We bring God to the world as we (2) "proclaim the excellencies of him who called [us] out of darkness into his marvelous light" (v. 9).

Peter does not explain what he means by "spiritual sacrifices." Paul uses the same imagery, however, to describe his ministry as apostle "in the priestly service of the gospel of God, so that the offering of the Gentiles may be acceptable, sanctified by the Holy Spirit" (Rom 15:16). For Paul—and presumably for Peter—including outsiders in God's family is what it meant to bring the world to God.

We bring God to the world, Peter tells us, by proclaiming his "excellencies" (v. 9). Verses 9–10 describe a community that simply cannot keep quiet about the goodness of God in our lives. We were once "not a people." We are now "God's people." Once we had "not received mercy." Now we "have received mercy." For Peter, proclaiming God's excellencies to others is simply the natural response to receiving God's mercy in our own lives.

The ensuing context, moreover, encourages us to understand "proclaim" (v. 9) in a sense that goes beyond the bare essentials of articulating the gospel, indeed, beyond words at all. Our whole lives are to broadcast the goodness of God to the world around us:

point. The notion of the whole people as a priesthood was not entirely new to the early Jewish Christians. God had designated Israel as a "kingdom of priests" when he delivered them from Egypt (Exod 19:6). The Israelites were to obey Torah, so that the surrounding nations would exclaim, "Surely this great nation is a wise and understanding people!" (Deut 4:6). In this sense, then, Israel as a whole stood in the gap between Yahweh and the nations.

What is new is the charge to "*Go* therefore and make disciples of all the nations" (Matt 28:19). The Old Testament restriction of God's presence to a local tabernacle (later, temple) meant that outsiders had to come to Israel in order to worship Yahweh (see Isa 56:6–7; Zech 8:20–23; 14:16–19). The Israelites could not bring God to them. Under the new covenant, God dwells in and among his people (1 Cor 3:15; 6:19; 2 Cor 6:16). Now, as we "go," we bring God to the world.

Missiologists distinguish, in this regard, between the centripetal nature of Israel's mission to the nations and the centrifugal orientation of Jesus's Great Commission. Jonah's mission to Nineveh was a rare old covenant exception to this pattern (Bauckham, *Bible and Mission*, 72–73).

Hands to the Plow Together

> Beloved, I urge you as sojourners and exiles to abstain from the passions of the flesh, which wage war against your soul. Keep your conduct among the Gentiles honorable, so that when they speak against you as evildoers, they may see your good deeds and glorify God on the day of visitation. (1 Pet 2:11–12)

There is some debate about the meaning of verse 12. The most reasonable interpretation takes the "day of visitation" to refer to the future return of Christ. The "Gentiles" ("pagans" [NIV]) can then be understood as persons who are initially antagonistic to the gospel but who turn to Christ in time to glorify God with the rest of the faithful when Jesus returns for his church. Peter traces the change of heart on the part of these unbelievers to the godliness and generosity of Christians whose behavior they have observed.

To proclaim God's excellencies, then, involves more than a verbal articulation of the gospel. We bring God to the world by how we live our lives, at home, at work, and at play—in short, by everything we say and do.

All Work Is Sacred

The implications are profound, especially for the average churchgoer. For the idea that we form a "holy priesthood" completely deconstructs the erroneous but common notion that the work of those who serve in vocational Christian ministry is somehow more meaningful than so-called secular employment.

The destructive notion of a hierarchy of vocations ultimately finds its origins in the pagan social hierarchy of antiquity, where manual labor was disdained by Greek and Roman elites. Its view of so-called secular labor is more Platonic—even gnostic—than Christian. A two-tiered system of priesthood and laity has plagued the church throughout history, despite the efforts during the Reformation to restore dignity and spiritual purpose to all human work.[12]

We learn from 1 Peter that my role as a pastor is no more "holy" or significant than that of my brothers and sisters who work in industry or

---

12. See the brief but helpful overview of the history of thinking about vocation in Chandler, *Christian Spiritual Formation*, 156–63, and the works cited there. I am attracted to Chandler's conceptualization of vocation as "being predicated on the love of God" and expressing itself fundamentally in "service to others for the glory of God" (161). For a more thorough treatment, see Veith, *God at Work*.

raise children in the home. And it is no more meaningful. All who name the name of Jesus are part of God's "holy priesthood," charged with bringing God to the world and the world to God. There is no life purpose more meaningful that this.

Staying the Course

According to the Florida Atlantic University study that we considered at the beginning of the chapter, a life of meaning and purpose helps significantly to insulate us from the symptoms of clinical depression. God has blessed his children with the most meaningful life imaginable. It ought to follow that Christians are the most emotionally healthy people on the planet.

We are not. Unfortunately, the inspiring picture Peter paints of our ministry as a royal priesthood has fallen on hard times, both among leaders and among those who serve in other capacities in our churches. The current state of leadership can serve as a litmus test of sorts for the spiritual health of the church at large.

Pastoral depression and burnout have become hot topics of conversation. The increasing demands of the job, along with the relational isolation that often characterizes a pastor's life, have generated some highly troubling trends:

- Forty percent of pastors and 47 percent of pastors' spouses are suffering from burnout, frantic schedules, and/or unrealistic expectations.
- Eighty percent of pastors believe that pastoral ministry affects their families negatively.
- Thirty-three percent of pastors say that being in ministry is an outright hazard to their family.
- Fifty-two percent of pastors say they and their spouses believe that being in pastoral ministry is hazardous to their family's well-being and health.
- Sixty-six percent of pastors and their families feel under pressure to model an ideal family.

Hands to the Plow Together

- Forty-five percent of pastors say that they've experienced depression or burnout to the extent that they have needed to take a leave of absence from ministry.
- Ninety percent of pastors feel unqualified or poorly prepared for ministry.
- Forty percent of pastors have considered leaving their pastorates in the past three months.
- Hundreds of pastors leave their ministries each month due to burnout, conflict, or moral failure.[13]

Volunteers in our communities are equally at risk. Churches recruit capable workers to run myriads of programs, often with little ongoing relational nurturing or support. The addition of ministry hours to an already full schedule of work and family tends to generate the same kind of stress and discouragement reported by vocational church workers.

Paul and the Challenges of Ministry

The apostle Paul's life and ministry have purpose and meaning written all over them. Paul never lost sight of the grandeur of his calling, even when he found himself in prison in Rome:

> To me, though I am the very least of all the saints, this grace was given, to preach to the Gentiles the unsearchable riches of Christ, and to bring to light for everyone what is the plan of the mystery hidden for ages in God who created all things, so that through the church the manifold wisdom of God might now be made known to the rulers and authorities in the heavenly places. This was according to the eternal purpose that he has realized in Christ Jesus our Lord, in whom we have boldness and access with confidence through our faith in him. (Eph 3:8–12)

Because of the perceived significance of his mission, moreover, Paul could reflect with great satisfaction upon his achievements:

> In Christ Jesus, then, I have reason to be proud of my work for God. For I will not venture to speak of anything except what

---

13. The statistics are taken from PastorBurnout.com/, "Pastor Burnout Statistics." The website draws from London and Wiseman, *Pastors at Greater Risk*, 20, 25–26, 148, 174–75.

> Christ has accomplished through me to bring the Gentiles to obedience—by word and deed, by the power of signs and wonders, by the power of the Spirit of God—so that from Jerusalem and all the way around to Illyricum I have fulfilled the ministry of the gospel of Christ. (Rom 15:17–19)

Yet the apostle Paul was no stranger to the difficulties of Christian ministry. He dealt with severe opposition from insiders and outsiders alike:

> Five times I received at the hands of the Jews the forty lashes less one. Three times I was beaten with rods. Once I was stoned. Three times I was shipwrecked; a night and a day I was adrift at sea; on frequent journeys, in danger from rivers, danger from robbers, danger from my own people, danger from Gentiles, danger in the city, danger in the wilderness, danger at sea, danger from false brothers; in toil and hardship, through many a sleepless night, in hunger and thirst, often without food, in cold and exposure. And, apart from other things, there is the daily pressure on me of my anxiety for all the churches. (2 Cor 11:24–28)

At one point Paul exclaims, "We were so utterly burdened beyond our strength that we despaired of life itself" (2 Cor 1:8).

We do not, however, see Paul experiencing the kind of personal emotional and spiritual crises reflected in the pastoral statistics listed above. Burnout was simply nowhere on the apostle's radar screen. Nor was depression.

Twice in 2 Corinthians Paul assures his readers "we do not lose heart" (4:1, 16). Several years later he uses the terms "joy" or "rejoice" fourteen times in a short letter written to the church in Philippi while he was incarcerated in Rome. Paul summarizes his outlook from prison in the last chapter of the letter:

> I have learned in whatever situation I am to be content. I know how to be brought low, and I know how to abound. In any and every circumstance, I have learned the secret of facing plenty and hunger, abundance and need. I can do all things through him who strengthens me. (Phil 4:11b–13)

Later, as his life draws to a close, Paul confidently claims, "I have fought the good fight, I have finished the race, I have kept the faith" (2 Tim 4:7).

Hands to the Plow Together

A Relational Approach to Service and Ministry

What can we learn from Paul about staying the course in ministry? About experiencing the joy of Christ in the midst of almost unrelenting people problems? About avoiding depression and burnout as we serve in the church?

Paul was one of a kind, so it is a bit unrealistic to set up the apostle to the Gentiles as a poster boy for everything spiritual in our lives today. Paul's calling and ministry were unique, and in some ways very different from yours and mine. At the very least, Paul did not have a family vying for his time and attention, as many of us do today.

Yet Paul exhorts us to imitate his life in Christ at several points in his letters (1 Cor 4:16; 11:1; Phil 3:17; 2 Thess 3:7, 9). Apparently some aspects of Paul's life and ministry should mark the experience of every follower of Jesus.

For starters, we would do well to imitate Paul's practice of serving God in community with others, whether we serve as leaders or followers. I am quite convinced that one of the keys to Paul's fulfilment and longevity in ministry was his commitment to minister as part of a team.

Many of us view Paul as a super-Christian of sorts, whose passion and gifts set him apart from his peers. From such a vantage point we too easily overlook the ways Paul was relationally connected with others in ministry.

Consider the portrait in Acts. Paul began his public ministry in Antioch, where he and Barnabas taught a great many people (11:26). Two chapters later we find Paul (still "Saul" in Luke's narrative) listed among a team of "prophets and teachers" in the church: "Barnabas, Simeon who was called Niger, Lucius of Cyrene, Manaen, a lifelong friend of Herod the tetrarch, and Saul" (13:1). Notice that Antioch lacked a single, authoritative leader responsible for the church's teachings. Several persons fed the flock (cf. 11:26; 13:1; 15:35).

The theme of team ministry continues in Acts with the missionary journeys. Paul partners on the first journey with Barnabas and John Mark (13:2, 5). "Paul and his companions," as Luke calls them (13:13), planted churches in Pisidian Antioch, Iconium, Lystra, and Derbe. On the second journey Paul associates at various times with Silas (15:36-40), Timothy (16:1-3), Luke (first-person plural verbs begin to appear at 16:10), and Priscilla and Aquila (18:1-3).

In between the two journeys, Antioch sent "Paul and Barnabas and some of the others" (15:2) to Jerusalem to debate the terms on which

Gentiles would be admitted to Christian community. Two of Jerusalem's leaders, Judas and Silas, accompanied the missionaries on their return trip to Antioch, where the four-man team related the apostles' decision (15:22, 30–31).

After they returned from the Jerusalem Council, Paul and Barnabas continued to minister together in Antioch, "teaching and preaching the word of the Lord, with many others also" (15:35). By way of summary, we note that local church ministry, missionary work, and conflict resolution were all community projects for the early Christians, according the Luke's narrative.

Paul's letters confirm the picture in Acts. Coworkers include Priscila and Aquila (Rom 16:3); Urbanus (Rom 16:9); Timothy (Rom 16:21; 1 Thess 3:2); Titus (2 Cor 8:23); Epaphroditus (Phil 2:25); Euodia, Syntyche, and Clement (Phil 4:2–3); Aristarchus, Mark, and Justus (Col 4:10–11; cf. Phlm 24); Philemon (Phlm 1); Demas; and Luke (Phlm 24).

It was not always easy for Paul to work as part of a team, and we should avoid idealizing Paul and his mission. The falling out with Barnabas in Acts 15:39 comes to mind. Team ministry is tough.

Paul's response to this relational breakdown with Barnabas, however, was not to go it alone. He immediately recruited Silas to accompany him on the second journey (Acts 15:40).

For Paul—arguably the greatest leader in church history—it was never "lonely at the top." The apostle consistently traveled and shared the ministry with his brothers and sisters in Christ. W.-H. Ollrog summarizes as follows:

> Paul explicitly calls no less than sixteen persons 'fellow workers,' and his usage, along with circumstantial evidence, suggests that he would have so identified another twenty to twenty-five women and men. Acts and the Pastorals have picked up this evidence and added another fifteen names. Paul's association with so many fellow workers has no parallel in early Christian missionary activity.[14]

Were the relationships Paul enjoyed with his coworkers a key to the apostle's robust optimism about his work for Christ and his staying power in ministry? Given the commonsense connection between healthy relationships on the one hand and human flourishing on the other, it could hardly have been otherwise.

---

14. Ollrog, "*Sunergos*," 3.304b.

Hands to the Plow Together

It is now axiomatic among those who study human longevity that persons engaged in healthy relationships generally live longer.[15] It only makes sense to assume that we will serve longer when we do so in community, as well.

The most troubling pastoral statistics in this regard may very well be the ones I left off the above list:

- Although 55 percent of pastors say they belong to a small accountability group, 70 percent claim they don't have any close friends.
- Fifty-six percent of pastors' wives say that they have no close friends.
- Twenty-five percent of pastors don't know where to turn when they have a family or personal conflict or issue; 20.5 percent say they would go to no one.[16]

No close friends. Nowhere to turn. Our lone-ranger approach to Christian leadership contrasts sharply with Paul's practice of ministering in community with others. And it is costing us dearly in terms of pastoral isolation, discouragement, and burnout.

I find myself deeply saddened when I think about the individual lives and families represented in these figures, in part because I find myself nowhere among the statistics.

Do I get discouraged at times? Seasons of exhaustion? Certainly. That's par for the course in the pastorate. But my family has flourished in vocational church ministry. Serious burnout has never been an issue. And I still cannot imagine doing anything else with my life.

I take no credit for any of this. By God's grace, Joann and I have never served alone. We began church work as part of a relationally healthy team of youth workers back in the late 1970s. A friend recruited me to co-pastor a church plant with him in 1996. I continue today at OCF serving on a team of eight pastors who share all facets of ministry and, more important, who share our lives together.

---

15. Bloom and Bloom, "Surprising Secret."

16. PastorBurnout.com/, "Pastor Burnout Statistics"; and London and Wiseman, *Pastors at Greater Risk*, 120, 164.

Conclusion

Once we have the physical necessities of food, clothing, shelter, and safety, our lives still need two ingredients in order for us to thrive as human beings: (1) a purpose for living; and (2) a place to belong, or, as one writer put it, significance and security.[17] God has wired us as human beings with a pressing sense of urgency to accomplish something meaningful with our lives. But he has also created us with "an inherent need to find safety and acceptance through relational attachment."[18]

God has met our need for purpose by commissioning us to be his agents of love and hope in a broken world. As we saw in 1 Peter 2, we find our greatest meaning in life when we function as a "royal priesthood" standing in the gap between God and a world that needs Jesus. There is no higher calling.

But God has not designed us to engage in this all-consuming adventure as isolated individuals. He intends for us to exercise this priestly calling in community with our brothers and sisters in Christ. Our purpose for living and our place to belong go together.[19]

The unfortunate experience of so many in our churches today—pastors and parishioners alike—testifies to the inescapable reality of this truth. Carefully review 1 Pet 2:4–10, above, and you will notice that all the descriptions are collective: "a spiritual house," "a holy priesthood," "a chosen race," "a royal priesthood," "a holy nation," "a people for his own possession." We are designed to engage in mission together, in community with others.

---

17. Crabb, *Basic Principles of Biblical Counseling*, 48–75.

18. Chandler, *Christian Spiritual Formation*, 112.

19. Anizor and Voss appropriately warn against "individualistic perversions of the priesthood of all believers" (*Representing Christ*, 104).

8

Lose the Story, Lose the Community

The Bible, Community, and Spiritual Formation

> Worship, at its most basic, is a celebration
> and a retelling of the story of God.
>
> —Kent Carlson[1]

IT HAS BEEN TRENDY in our postmodern culture to emphasize what we cannot know about God over against what we can know about him. Brian McLaren's observations are representative:

> When we 'do theology,' we are clay pots pondering the potter, kids pondering their father, ants discussing the elephant. At some level of profundity and accuracy, we are bound to be inadequate or incomplete all the time, in almost everything we say or think, considering our human limitations, including language, and God's infinite greatness.[2]

Comments like these appropriately remind us of the limitations of the modernist epistemologies that have dominated theological studies since the Enlightenment. We can be overly optimistic about how much we can know about God.

But we can be overly pessimistic too, and here McLaren has significantly overplayed his hand. Consider his analogy of "ants discussing the elephant." D. A. Carson insightfully reminds us that the comparison "overlooks the fact that in this case the ants have been made in the image of

---

1. Carlson and Lueken, *Renovation of the Church*, 149.
2. McLaren, *Church on the Other Side*, 65.

the elephant, and *this elephant has not only communicated with the ants in ant-language*, but has also, in the person of the Son, become an "ant" while remaining an 'elephant.'"³ The italicized statement is the one I want us to focus on here. By "ant-language," Carson refers, of course, to the inspired text of Scripture. As it turns out, the story of redemption narrated in the Bible is closely related to the theme of spiritual formation in community that has dominated this book.⁴

Communities and stories go together. Members of a community rely on a defining narrative to provide a sense of communal identity and to establish group boundaries. This is why God instructed the Israelites to tell the story of Passover to their children whenever they celebrated the festival:

> And when your children say to you, "What do you mean by this service?" you shall say, "It is the sacrifice of the LORD's Passover, for he passed over the houses of the people of Israel in Egypt, when he struck the Egyptians but spared our houses." (Exod 12:26–27)

God wanted his people to know who they were and to appreciate their unique identity vis-à-vis the surrounding nations. This would only happen if the Israelites remembered the story of the Egyptian exodus and faithfully handed down their defining narrative from generation to generation.

A Storied Universe: The Ubiquity of Stories in Our Lives

For many of us the word *story* conjures up memories of the short stories and novels we read for our English classes in high school or college. Few of us read much anymore, maybe twenty minutes per day on the average. Nevertheless, we spend the majority of our waking and sleeping hours living in a storied universe. Story, as it turns out, is much bigger than the printed (or pixeled) word.

---

3. Carson, *Becoming Conversant*, 129.

4. This chapter broadly considers the function of Scripture as story and its contribution to Christian communal solidarity. For the role of the Bible in personal spiritual formation (SF), see Russell, *Playing with Fire*, and Mulholland, *Shaped by the Word*. Langer offers some important correctives to the way in which some proponents of SF have approached the Bible ("Points of Unease," 202–5).

Lose the Story, Lose the Community

Storied Playtime

Our attraction to story begins early in life. When my daughters were young, Beanie Babies were the rage. Children played with them, adults collected them, and Ty Incorporated made millions manufacturing and selling them. Rebekah and Rachel spent hours creating whole scenarios with their Beanies.

The Hellerman Beanies lived together in a town. Lulu the duck served as the town's first female mayor. Snip the Cat and Doby the Dog ran an ice cream shop. Another Beanie dog operated "Rover's Love Connection." Rover was the town's matchmaker and specialist in conflict resolution.

Crisis was the norm. The local grammar school was full of drama among doting parents. Patti the platypus did not want her daughter to play with Weedle and Waddle, because the penguin twins misbehaved. Beanies went under the surgeon's knife at the local hospital to have their tags removed. One year, when the Summer Olympics were on television in the living room, the Beanie Baby Olympics were unfolding in the girls' room, with accompanying backstories that rivaled anything NBC could produce.

There was even a Beanie Baby holocaust. The brand-name Beanies tried to eliminate all the knockoffs that Rebekah and Rachel had acquired. Toughie the Terrier, the instigator of the pogrom, went to prison for war crimes.

This is not unique to my daughters. Children everywhere occupy a storied universe virtually every time they play, alone or together with others.

Storied Media

Our love for stories does not end with childhood. The time that Americans spend in the front of the television, in movie theaters, and watching videos adds up to a whopping 1,900 hours per year (five hours per day). Virtually all of this time is story time.

Story propels sitcoms, soap operas, movies, and the like. In a less obvious way, story also functions as the setting for newscasts, documentaries, sports—even commercials. The bare facts that these programs purport to relate almost always find themselves embedded in a backstory that situates the data in a narrative context to captivate viewers.

Consider the Olympics. We are inundated with biographical backstories that portray an athlete's sixty-second performance as the culmination of two decades of life and relationships. Instead of a bare act of athletic prowess, that final run down the mountain becomes the tension-filled climax to a downhill skier's life story of personal dreams, struggles, and now, hopefully, triumph.

Who can forget the drama surrounding Nancy Kerrigan and Tonya Harding at the 1994 Winter Olympics? The competition itself became the climactic scene of a melodrama that had begun months earlier, when Harding's ex-husband and her bodyguard hired a thug to break Kerrigan's leg (he managed only to severely bruise her) so that she would be unable to compete against Harding in the Olympics.

Even the news depends on story to keep our interest. Recently, in California, a FedEx truck careered across the center divider of Interstate 5 and collided head-on with a bus. Ten people (including both drivers) were killed and a dozen more injured. Those are the bare facts. But bare facts are not enough. We want more. We want the backstory.

Who was on that bus? Where was it headed?

The bus carried a group of underprivileged inner-city high school kids from the Los Angeles Unified High School District. They were scheduled to tour Humboldt State University. Students who died in the accident would have been the first members of their families to attend college.

Over the next few days came interviews with families and friends of the young people who perished, along with other information typically generated in the media by such an event. Bare facts became a story—a very sad story, but a story nonetheless.

Storied Dreaming

Dreams are stories too, though often rather bizarre ones. We used to think we dreamed only during REM sleep cycles, which still would have us "spontaneously scripting and screening night stories in the theaters of [our] minds" about two hours per night.[5] Sleep researchers now know that narrative dreaming occurs throughout the night, across the whole sleep cycle.

We dream when we are awake too—a whole lot more than most of us realize. Recent studies find us spending about half our waking hours daydreaming. Daydreaming is the mind's default state: "We daydream when driving, when walking, when cooking dinner, when getting dressed

---

5. Gottschall, *Storytelling Animal*, 10. I am indebted to Gottschall for much of what follows.

in the morning, when staring off into space at work. In short, whenever the mind is not absorbed in a mentally demanding task—say writing a paragraph like this one or doing some difficult calculations—it will get restless and skip off into la-la land."[6]

We could go on and on, with the stories in the songs we listen to, the stories that frame the commercials we watch, the stories triggered in our minds when we glance at a tabloid at the grocery store, and so forth. But I trust you get the picture.

In *The Gates of the Forest*, Elie Wiesel wrote, "God made Man because He loves stories."[7] He could as easily have written, "God made Man *to love* stories." Human beings are storytelling animals.

Wired for Story: The Function of Stories in Our Lives

Why are we wired to spend the majority of our waking and sleeping hours living in a storied universe? Literary theorists and evolutionary psychologists offer various explanations. Jonathan Gottschall suggests that "the human mind was shaped *for* story, so that it could be shaped *by* story."[8] I believe he is right, although I would trace the phenomenon to the Creator's intelligent design, rather than (with Gottschall) to an evolutionary process of natural selection.

What is indisputable is that stories function as powerful change agents in our lives. We do not go away from our stories untouched.

The Microfunction of Stories: Stories and Personal Morality

When Christians think of the influence of media on morals, what often comes to mind are images of sex and violence, and the ongoing debates about how much these images influence real-life behavior. The relationship between virtual reality and life is actually much more subtle. For it is the stories in which these images are embedded—not simply the images themselves—that do the heavy lifting of making and molding the moral values of the viewers.

---

6. Ibid., 11.
7. Wiesel, *Gates of the Forest*, preface.
8. Ibid., 56.

Preoccupation with isolated media images and events has obscured the general pattern of conventional moralizing that characterizes most storytelling. Violence in the media is rarely gratuitous. Rather, it functions within the context of narratives that are strongly marked by poetic justice: "When the villain kills, his or her violence is condemned. When the hero kills, he or she does so righteously. Fiction drives home the message that violence is acceptable only under clearly defined circumstances—to protect the good and the weak from the bad and the strong."[9] There are certainly exceptions. But as a general rule, fiction "puts us in the position of approving of decent, prosocial behavior and disapproving of the greed of antagonists—of characters who are all belly and balls."[10]

We do not walk away from this ubiquitous moralizing unaffected. Consider Markus Appel's 2008 study of "just-world" beliefs. In the real world, it is simply a fact that bad things often happen to good people and that most crimes go unpunished. The majority of us, however, believe otherwise. We somehow assume that justice will have its way. The bad guy will get what is coming to him and virtue will be rewarded.

Where do we get these convictions? Primarily from the stories we are told. The Appel study found that people who viewed mostly drama and comedy on TV rather than news and documentaries had significantly stronger "just-world" beliefs.

Well-crafted stories—from the sweeping narratives of the world's religions to TV shows to children's fairy tales—consistently immerse us in themes of poetic justice, where virtue is rewarded and vice is condemned. The result? We begin to believe, in the face of real-life evidence to the contrary, that the world is a just place.

The world is, in fact, a just place in the grand eschatological scheme of things, from a Christian perspective. But for society to function in an orderly way, people need to have confidence that justice will prevail in the here and now, on this side of eternity.

We need to buy into the "just-world" beliefs imparted by our stories. Otherwise, why act justly in our relations with others? The microfunction of story to mold personal morality thus affects the relational values of our social world. This leads us to consider the macrofunction of story: to reinforce communal values and social identity.

---

9. Ibid., 132.
10. Ibid.

Lose the Story, Lose the Community

The Macrofunction of Stories: Stories and Communal Solidarity

One of the primary functions of story and storytelling in human life is to establish and maintain social boundaries and group solidarity. Narratives define and reinforce communal identity, whether a group is large or small.

Included in our church's New Members' Workbook is a five-page history of OCF. Newcomers learn about the birth of our church in a home meeting in 1986, and we walk them through a series of defining community events that occurred in the years that followed. We want newcomers to understand who we are so that they will know who they will become if they join our church. Sharing "The OCF Story" has been an effective way to accomplish this.

On a broader scale, social anthropologists inform us that nearly every people group has a defining story or cluster of stories that serves to reinforce a collective awareness of its common origins. This shared history functions "to maintain group cohesiveness, sustain and enhance identity, and to establish social networks and communicative patterns."[11] Included are stories "of origin; of migration and liberation; of descent; of an heroic age; of communal decline, conquest, and exile; and of rebirth, with a summons to action."[12]

Examples abound. The shared consciousness of African Americans owes much to the unfolding story of American slavery, the Civil War, and the civil rights movement of the 1960s. Memories of the Armenian genocide perpetrated by Ottoman Turks in the early twentieth century continue to play strongly into the sense of social solidarity shared among Armenian communities around the world today.

Ancient Israelites retold the story of the exodus every year at Passover. Dozens of narratives from elsewhere in the Hebrew Scriptures were heard regularly in synagogues in first-century Palestine. Jews today continue to tell these stories, along with a more recent story of origins that has become the defining narrative for the modern nation of Israel and for many non-Israeli Jews, as well.

The enduring solidarity of a social group is directly related (a) to the power of its story of origins and (b) to how effectively that story is communicated to future generations. In June 2013, my wife and I spent an afternoon in Yad Vashem, the Holocaust museum in Jerusalem. This

---

11. Patterson, "Context and Choice," 305.
12. Gurr and Harff, *Ethnic Conflict*, 12–13.

remarkable story-in-stone consists of a stark, concrete building that gradually descends an incline, as visitors pass from displays depicting the rise of Nazi Germany in early twentieth-century Europe to graphic images and material remains of the horrors of Buchenwald and Auschwitz at the museum's point of lowest elevation.

An ascent back to ground level follows, which portrays increasingly positive images of the birth of modern Israel in 1948 and ensuing events in the growth of this extraordinary Middle Eastern democracy. The alignment of the vivid displays with the physical descent and ascent of the minimalist structure makes for an extremely moving experience for museum guests.

In 2006 Yad Vashem established a new Study Center for Youth in order to ensure that every Israeli high schooler would spend a day at the museum, as part of an eleventh-grade study of the Holocaust. The power of the defining narrative of the Holocaust followed by the rebirth of Israel—and the effectiveness of Yad Vashem in socializing new generations of Israelis to embrace it—goes a long way to explain the cohesiveness, resourcefulness, and national consciousness that Israelis share today.

Our brief digression into the field of social anthropology has not been without design. The macrofunction of stories to socialize humans to identify with a community and its values has profound implications for Christian spiritual formation.

If, as I argued earlier, spiritual growth occurs primarily in the context of Christian community, then the Bible, as story, becomes central to the maturation process. For if, as Jonathan Gottschall maintains, story is "a form of social glue that brings people together around common values," then the story of redemption—as narrated in Scripture—is the "glue" that keeps God's people "together." And we must remain together to grow in our Christian lives.

The Challenge of Competing Narratives

Today the story of the Bible must vigorously compete to retain pride of place among a myriad of stories that are seeking to establish and reinforce other, very different, views of the world.

Some things never change. As storytelling animals we are still engaged in "a socially regulating activity." But modern media has utterly transformed the socialization process—and not in a way that should encourage those of us seeking to grow in the grace and knowledge of our Lord Jesus Christ.

Lose the Story, Lose the Community

Gottschall's observations about the socializing power of media warrant extended quotation:

> In recent centuries, technology has changed the communal nature of story, but it has not destroyed it. Nowadays we may imbibe most of our stories alone or with our families and our friends, but we are still engaged in a socially regulating activity. I may be by myself watching *Breaking Bad* or *30 Rock*, or reading *The Da Vinci Code* or *The Girl with the Dragon Tattoo*, but there are millions of other people sitting on millions of other couches being exposed to exactly the same stories and undergoing exactly the same process of neural, emotional, and physiological attunement. We are still having a communal experience; it's just spread out over space and time.
>
> Story, in other words, continues to fulfill its ancient function of binding society by reinforcing a set of common values and strengthening the ties of common culture. Story enculturates the youth. It defines the people. It tells us what is laudable and what is contemptible.[13]

We have experienced this very phenomenon in recent decades in American life. In 2003, 58 percent of the American public was opposed to allowing gays and lesbians to marry legally. Only a third (33 percent) favored same-sex marriage. Ten years later a 2013 survey by the Pew Research Center, conducted among 1,501 adults nationwide, found 49 percent supporting same-sex marriage, and 44 percent opposed.

Given the power of story to determine community values, it is hardly coincidental that our society's change in convictions about gay marriage followed right on the heels of increasing media portrayals of homosexuality in a positive light.

Until the 1990s there was a relative absence of gay characters on television. The 1997–1998 season had sixteen shows with leading or recurring gay characters. In three short years that number almost doubled, to twenty-nine shows in the 2000–2001 season. It is now virtually obligatory for every sitcom to feature a gay character as part of its storytelling.

The Bible is our defining narrative. God intends for the comprehensive story of creation, fall, redemption, and restoration to bind us together so that we can make progress in the faith. But the story of God's people as revealed in Scripture is in danger of being overwhelmed by the torrent of stories we encounter in the media and elsewhere in our daily lives. At the

13. Gottschall, *Storytelling Animal*, 137–38.

same time, evangelicals are becoming increasingly biblically illiterate. What happens when a people loses touch with its defining narrative?

Lose the Story, and You Lose the Community

The summer of 2012 saw the debut of a book titled *Still the Best Hope: Why the World Needs American Values to Triumph*, by Dennis Prager.[14] Back in the 1950s–1960s, when I went through the public schools, a book like Prager's would not have seen the light of day, because none of us needed any convincing that America was *Still the Best Hope*.

The U.S.A. had recently delivered the world from the threats of Nazi Germany and imperial Japan. We were currently in the middle of the Cold War. The Communists were the bad guys. Americans were the good guys. We Americans all inhabited the same story. That story defined us and bound us together.

Then came the assassination of the Kennedy brothers. Vietnam. Watergate. Enron. The sexual revolution. Multiculturalism. The postmodern deconstruction of metanarratives.

Competing stories about America began to replace the stories I had heard in grammar school. Some were disturbing. The slaughter of Native Americans. The oppression of African Americans through slavery and Jim Crow laws. Revisionist historians such as Howard Zinn and James Loewen began to craft a very different history of the United States, asserting that the *Lies My Teacher Told Me* hopelessly idealized America's past so as to almost completely obscure what really happened.[15]

Today America has lost much of its unifying narrative. Given what we know about the function of shared national myths to engender a collective consciousness for a people, it is hardly surprising that America's sense of social solidarity has been compromised, as well. Red states and blue states, the polarization of the Left and the Right, culture wars—*E pluribus unum* is becoming harder and harder to maintain.

Whether we find this regrettable or refreshing is not the point in the present connection. What I want us to notice is how a society's social fabric begins to tear when its defining narrative is deconstructed. Lose the story and you lose the community.

---

14. Prager, *Still the Best Hope*.
15. Loewen, *Lies My Teacher Told Me*; Zinn, *A People's History*.

Losing Our Story: The Challenge of Biblical Illiteracy

With all due respect to Dennis Prager, America is not *The Best Hope*. It never was. Jesus is the best hope, for us and for the world. But we can only live in the light of the hope Jesus offers—and bring this hope to the world—if we are living our lives within the story of the people of God, as it unfolds in the Bible.

If statistics about biblical literacy among evangelicals are any indication, we are in danger of losing our story.[16] Sadly, many Christians I know seem to be more concerned about the deconstruction of America's traditional unifying narrative than they are about the decline of interest in the defining narrative of Scripture in our churches today.

Biblical literacy is particularly on the wane among younger evangelicals. A 2004 Gallup poll found that nearly 60 percent of American teens who self-identified as evangelical were not able to correctly identify Cain as the one who said, "Am I my brother's keeper?" More than half could not identify "Blessed are the poor in spirit" as a quote from the Sermon on the Mount. When faced with these and similar questions, evangelical teens fared only slightly better than their nonevangelical counterparts.

Here, however, the devil is decidedly not in the details. More problematic than unfamiliarity with the specific data points of Scripture is an even more widespread ignorance of the Bible's overarching narrative. If David Nienhuis's anecdotal survey of students at Seattle Pacific University is any indication, we may have already lost our story.[17]

Nienhuis begins his Bible survey course by asking students to take a biblical literacy quiz. Ninety-five percent of his students are Christians. Half attend evangelical churches. As part of the quiz, Nienhuis requests that students "sequence major stories and events from the biblical metanarrative." Only 23 percent were able accurately to order four key Old Testament events:

1. Israelites enter the promised land
2. David is made king
3. Israel is divided in two

---

16. See the 2013 Barna Group study commissioned by the American Bible Society: Barna Group, "State of the Bible 2013." The study surveys the general population but reflects similar trends among American evangelicals.

17. Nienhuis, "Problem of Biblical Illiteracy," 11.

4. Judah goes into exile

A mere 32 percent were able to sequence four important New Testament events:

1. Jesus was baptized
2. Peter denies Jesus
3. The Spirit descends at Pentecost
4. John has a vision on the island of Patmos

It is difficult to see how a story that we can no longer tell as Christians can in any way continue to function as "a form of social glue" that brings us together "around common values."[18] Lose the story and you lose the community.

A Verse Here, a Verse There

Even when we do focus on biblical literacy, evangelicals traditionally underemphasize the overarching narrative of Scripture. Instead, we encourage "the memorization of discrete Bible verses and 'facts,' mostly in the service of evangelism and apologetics."[19] As Nienhuis notes,

> this method leads students to uncritically assume that doctrinal reflection is exhausted by the capacity to quote a much-loved proof-text. In doing this they suppose not only that the passage they are quoting is entirely perspicuous as it stands (in complete isolation from its literary and historical context), but also that the cited text is capable of performing as a summary of the entire biblical witness on the matter at hand.[20]

Compounding the problem is the selective nature of our proof-texting. We do not choose our favorite verses from a position of theological neutrality. The preference for certain verses to the exclusion of others is often determined by current cultural values rather than by the priorities of the biblical story as a whole.

The result an atomistic, nonnarrative approach to the Bible that renders us particularly vulnerable to the influence of culture upon our understanding

---

18. Gottschall, *Storytelling Animal*, 137–38.
19. Nienhuis, "Problem of Biblical Illiteracy," 13.
20. Ibid.

Lose the Story, Lose the Community

of the Christian life. The preoccupation of American evangelicals with our personal relationship with God—contrasted with the biblical focus on church community as the primary context for Christian formation—constitutes but one regrettable effect of this phenomenon.

Find the Story, and You Find the Community

On at least two occasions the biblical narrative itself colorfully illustrates the inseparable connection between story and communal identity. As we saw at the beginning of the chapter, God intended for the Israelites to remember their story of origins and to retell it to every generation. Israel, however, neglected to do this. They lost their story, they compromised with pagan religion, and, as a result, they lost their sense of identity as the chosen people of God.

Josiah Finds God's Story

As Israel's history unfolded, it was not long before "everyone did what was right in his own eyes" (Judg 17:6; 21:25). Later, during the monarchy, king after king did "evil in the sight of the Lord" (1 Kgs 11:16; 15:26, 34; 16:19, 25, 30; 21:20, 25; 22:52; 2 Kgs 3:2; 8:18, 27; 13:2, 11; 14:24; 15:9, 18, 24, 28; 17:2; 17:17; 21:2, 6, 20). By the middle of the seventh-century BCE, things had gotten so bad that Judah's King Manasseh (c. 687–642 BC) "burned his sons as an offering in the Valley of the Son of Hinnom" (2 Chr 33:6).

A remarkable series of events then began to unfold. The Israelites found their story and, correspondingly, they regained their sense of community.

It happened during the reign of Manasseh's grandson Josiah (c. 641–609 BCE). For generations no one had heard the narrative of Israel's history. Then a priest stumbled upon a long-lost copy of the law of Moses and passed it on to the king. The biblical story had quite an effect on Josiah and his subjects: "When the king heard the words of the Book of the Law, he tore his clothes" (2 Kgs 22:11).

> And the king went up to the house of the Lord, and with him all the men of Judah and all the inhabitants of Jerusalem and the priests and the prophets, all the people, both small and great. And he read in their hearing all the words of the Book of the Covenant that had been found in the house of the Lord. And the king stood by the pillar and made a covenant before the Lord, to walk after

> the LORD and to keep his commandments and his testimonies and his statutes with all his heart and all his soul, to perform the words of this covenant that were written in this book. And all the people joined in the covenant. (2 Kgs 23:2–3)

Josiah then cleansed the land of Baal worship and all forms of pagan religion (2 Kgs 23:4–20). The revival culminated in the observance of the feast of Passover. It was the first time in years that the Israelites collectively celebrated their defining narrative of the exodus from Egypt and their constitution as a people of Yahweh at Sinai:

> And the king commanded all the people, "Keep the Passover to the LORD your God, as it is written in this Book of the Covenant." For no such Passover had been kept since the days of the judges who judged Israel, or during all the days of the kings of Israel or of the kings of Judah. But in the eighteenth year of King Josiah this Passover was kept to the LORD in Jerusalem. (2 Kgs 23:21–23)

Ezra Tells God's Story

We encounter another striking example of the power of God's story to reinforce community during the postexilic period. Jewish leaders who returned to Judah from Babylon (in the sixth century BCE) found their fellow Jews on the verge of losing their social identity as God's chosen people. Shortly after Ezra arrived in Jerusalem, officials informed him,

> The people of Israel and the priests and the Levites have not separated themselves from the peoples of the lands with their abominations, from the Canaanites, the Hittites, the Perizzites, the Jebusites, the Ammonites, the Moabites, the Egyptians, and the Amorites. (Ezra 9:1)

Particularly troublesome was intermarriage with non-Jews:

> They have taken some of their daughters to be wives for themselves and for their sons, so that the holy race has mixed itself with the peoples of the lands. (Ezra 9:2a)

The practice had become so widespread that "half of their children spoke the language of Ashdod, and they could not speak the language of Judah" (Neh 13:24).

Lose the Story, Lose the Community

Most culpable were Judah's leaders: "in this faithlessness the hand of the officials and chief men has been foremost" (Ezra 9:2b). Eliashib the priest had apparently brokered a family relationship with Israel's enemy, Tobiah the Ammonite, and set Tobiah up with a nicely furnished apartment right in the temple courts (Neh 13:7).

Once again, the defining narrative of Scripture served as the primary catalyst to remind the Israelites of their social identity as the holy people of God. It all began with a couple weeks of serious Bible reading and study:

> All the people gathered as one man into the square before the Water Gate. And they told Ezra the scribe to bring the Book of the Law of Moses that the LORD had commanded Israel. So Ezra the priest brought the Law before the assembly, both men and women and all who could understand what they heard, on the first day of the seventh month. And he read from it facing the square before the Water Gate from early morning until midday, in the presence of the men and the women and those who could understand. And the ears of all the people were attentive to the Book of the Law. (Neh 8:1–3)

On the following day Jerusalem's leaders "came together to Ezra the scribe in order to study the words of the Law" (Neh 8:13). They encountered a passage in the Torah describing the Feast of Booths and decided to observe the festival. During the celebration, Ezra spent another seven days reading to the people "the Book of the Law of God" (Neh 8:18).

Israel rediscovered her story. This renewed commitment to Scripture, in turn, powerfully rekindled their sense of communal identity. Find your story and you will find your community:

> As soon as the people heard the law, they separated from Israel all those of foreign descent. (Neh 13:3)

Tobiah the Ammonite was among the first to receive his eviction notice:

> "I threw all the household furniture of Tobiah out of the chamber. Then I gave orders, and they cleansed the chambers, and I brought back there the vessels of the house of God, with the grain offering and the frankincense." (Neh 13:8–9)

The Old Testament experiences of Josiah and Ezra show what happens when the people of God rediscover their defining narrative. In each case the Israelites found their story. And they once again found their community.

Conclusion

We grow spiritually only when we are in community with our brothers and sisters in Christ. This has been the repeated refrain of the book. What, then, is a chapter about the Bible doing in a book about community and spiritual formation?

I trust that the answer to that question has become quite clear. A community rises and falls with the vitality of its defining narrative. In the words of Jonathan Gottschall, "Story—sacred and profane—is perhaps the main cohering force in human life."[21]

What a story we have! The Bible tells the story of a God who created us for his glory, who restored us when we rebelled, and who has placed us in a community with a mission big enough to capture the hearts and minds of every human being on this planet.

The story is not the problem. Effectively communicating it—especially to future generations—is the pressing task at hand. Lose the story, and you lose the community. And American evangelicals are increasingly in danger of losing our story.

The enduring solidarity of the Christian church as a healthy context for spiritual formation will depend for its future upon an intentional recommitment to biblical literacy, reflected in a renewed determination to pass on the defining narrative of Scripture to our younger brothers and sisters in the faith. We must find our story once again.

The challenges are not insignificant. But neither are they insurmountable. David Nienhuis's prescription for a return to biblical literacy will serve as an apt conclusion to our consideration of the inseparable connection between story, community, and spiritual formation. Nienhuis sees the task ahead of us as threefold:

1. Schooling in the substance of the entire biblical story in all its literary diversity.

2. Training in the particular "orienteering" skills required to plot that narrative through the actual texts and canonical units of the Bible.

3. Instruction in the complex theological task of interpreting Scripture in light of the tradition of the church and the experience of the saints.[22]

---

21. Gottschall, *Storytelling Animal*, 137–38.
22. Nienhaus, "The Problem of Biblical Illiteracy," 13.

Lose the Story, Lose the Community

As American social life becomes increasingly post-Christian, it is imperative that we intentionally situate God's Story at the center of the educational ministry of the church and of our individual lives.[23]

---

23. For an informative and inspiring challenge along these lines, see Berding. *Bible Revival.*

9

Until Jesus Returns

Eschatology and Spiritual Formation

> "Does this hope cheat man of the happiness of the present? How could it do so! For it is itself the happiness of the present."
>
> —Jürgen Moltmann[1]

Most evangelicals think of eschatology as the area of biblical studies that deals with events surrounding the future return of Jesus Christ. Rightly so, since the second coming is a major theme of the New Testament. But the future is only one part of the biblical eschatological picture.

The early Christians also believed and taught that the eschaton had already begun, that "the arrival of Jesus the Messiah has brought the end into the 'now' of human history."[2] The kingdom of God was inaugurated in the coming of the Son (cf. Mark 1:15) and continues, after Pentecost, in the reign of the Spirit in the church (Acts 2).

Thus in the first Christian sermon, Peter informs his audience that they have already entered "the last days" (cf. Acts 2:16–17). Theologians rightly speak, therefore, of an "already" and a "not yet" aspect of the kingdom of God.

It is not hard to see how the "already" aspect of the kingdom—now epitomized in the presence of the Spirit in the church—might have something to do with spiritual life and growth. It is more difficult to see how the "not yet" part of God's program might inform the topic.

---

1. Moltmann, *Theology of Hope*, 32.
2. Brown et al., *Becoming Whole*, 76.

Many of us find it hard to connect the future with the present. I suspect that this is why so few churches teach and preach anymore about what God has in store for the future. We are preoccupied with the here and now. And we are not convinced that the future has much to say to us about our day-to-day lives. The second coming is then. Spiritual formation is now.

This disconnect is unfortunate, for as Kyle Roberts observes, "Christian spirituality depends on hope for its survival."³ The New Testament repeatedly and forcefully points to the return of Christ as a key reason to remain faithful and continue to grow in Christ in the here-and-now.

Indeed, Scripture portrays God's "already" as the proleptic experience—in our present lives—of the "not yet" that is still to come. We have "the firstfruits of the Spirit" (Rom 8:23), who is "the pledge of our inheritance" (Eph 1:14)—thus the common description of the current stage of salvation history as a time of "inaugurated" eschatology.⁴

Both the "already" and the "not yet" aspects of the kingdom of God have much to say about our progress in the Christian life. We will look first at God's "already." The bulk of the chapter will then focus more extensively on future eschatology, since this central New Testament theme is currently deemphasized—much to our detriment—in the evangelical community.⁵

The Reign of the Holy Spirit: God's "Already"

The earlier chapters of this book, dealing with community and spiritual formation, tacitly assumed the reality of the "already" aspect of the kingdom. Let us now consider more directly the significance of what we might call a partially realized eschatology for our progress in the faith.

As a point of departure, I will use "kingdom," in the phrase "kingdom of God," as a dynamic and not a static term. "Kingdom" in the New Testament is most often the *exercise* of kingly rule, not the place where God

---

3. Roberts, "Eschatology and Hope," 88.

4. For a helpful discussion of the continuity between this age and the age to come, see Haas, "Significance of Eschatology." A more thorough treatment of the topic can be found in Beale, "Eschatological Conception," which discusses in some detail the "Already" of New Testament eschatology.

5. By future eschatology I am not referring to dispensationalist end-time scenarios purporting to align biblical prophecy with current events in the Middle East. We have stood around long enough "looking into the sky" (Acts 1:11). What I have in mind, rather, is the ubiquitous biblical use of the future hope of Christ's return as a motivator for faithfulness and progress in our Christian lives.

rules. Thus Jesus proclaims, "If it is by the Spirit of God that I cast out demons, then the kingdom of God has come upon you" (Matt 12:28; par. Luke 11:20). Jesus speaks here of the effective rule or reign of God, not a geopolitical realm of some sort.

Mark Saucy has recently equated the "already" of God's kingdom program, as we see it unfold in the New Testament, with the reign of the Holy Spirit, first in the life of Jesus of Nazareth and then in his body, the church. The Spirit is "the locus of kingdom power in the present age."[6] And Jesus, as portrayed in the Gospels, becomes "the prototype of such spiritual formation processes that the apostles bear witness to in their NT writings."[7]

Robert Muholland similarly identifies the Spirit as the agent through whom Christians are spiritually formed. Transformation consists of "being nurtured and restored to wholeness in the image of God through a growing relationship of loving union with God in Christ *through the Holy Spirit*" (cf. 2 Cor 3:18).[8]

But just how does this occur? Can we be more specific regarding the transforming role of the Spirit in our lives? Saucy offers some helpful insights along these lines when he enumerates "three loci of the Spirit-kingdom's present activity for spiritual formation":[9]

1. The Spirit empowers us to announce, and enables us to apprehend, the grace of forgiveness.

2. The Spirit compels us toward greater submission to the Lordship of Christ and away from slavery to rival "lords."

3. The Spirit unites us with others in community.

While surely less than exhaustive, Saucy's threefold template offers a relatively robust picture of the role of the Holy Spirit in the process of Christian maturation.

When we become Christians, we enter into new life in the Spirit (#1, above), where we are (a) empowered to proclaim the good news of forgiveness to others and (b) enabled by the Spirit to apprehend the "graced" state of

---

6. Saucy, "*Regnum Spiriti*," 147. I will interact with Saucy's discussion in what follows.

7. Ibid., 144.

8. Mulholland, "Spirituality and Transformation," 218 (italics added). Davis, *Meditation and Communion with God*, explores the implications of inaugurated eschatology for God's presence in the reading of Scripture.

9. Saucy, "*Regnum Spiriti*," 149–53. On the role of the Spirit in spiritual formation, see also Bock, "New Testament Community and Spiritual Formation," 105–8.

our own relationship with God. As we grow in our understanding of God's unconditional acceptance, we trade a self-referenced life for a God-referenced identity and thereby become increasingly "free to come out from hiding in the shadows of our moralism and be wholly genuine and real."[10]

Progress in the spiritual life also involves greater submission to Jesus as Lord (#2, above). This too is the work of the Spirit of God in our lives. It manifests itself as we align ourselves with God's priorities and experience increasing victory over the competing domains of the flesh, the world, and the devil.

Finally, a spiritually formed person will persevere with others in the fellowship of Christ's church (#3, above). This point dovetails nicely with the discussion of community in chapters 1–5. Indeed, as it turns out, the first two activities of the Spirit listed above depend upon the third for their effectiveness. Saucy's conclusion warrants extended quotation:

> It is when the body of Christ dwells in unity bonded by the power of the Spirit for mutual love [(#3, above)] that it enjoys the means of proclamation to the world of the redeeming power of forgiveness in Christ (John 13:35 [#1, above]). It is also in this kind of community that believers together grow in their own apprehension of God's gracious acceptance as they see it reflected in the deeds of love and forgiveness of their brothers and sisters. Finally, it is in the Spirit-formed community that Christ's unique lordship for each one is pursued and defended most effectively [(#2)].[11]

In these important ways, then, "spiritual formation as the product of the Spirit's work is not an *individual* quest, but more of a *corporate one*."[12]

So much for our present relationship with God through his Spirit. We turn now to consider the "not yet" of God's eschatological program.

Eyes on the Prize: God's "Not Yet"

According to the New Testament, we are *empowered* to live for Jesus by the presence of the Holy Spirit in our lives (Rom 8:1–17; Gal 5:16–23). We are *motivated* to do so (a) by what God has done in the past and (b) by what

---

10. Saucy, "*Regnum Spiriti*," 151. The expressions "self-referenced" and "God-referenced" are from Mulholland, "Spirituality and Transformation," 218–19. Saucy and Mulholland use different language to say much the same thing.

11. Saucy, "*Regnum Spiriti*," 153. I have added [point 1], [point 2], and [point 3].

12. Ibid., 152 (italics original).

God will do in the future. Past, present, and future each find a place in Paul's robust description of the Christian life in Titus 2:11–14:

> For the grace of God has appeared, bringing salvation for all people, training us to renounce ungodliness and worldly passions, and to live self-controlled, upright, and godly lives in the present age, waiting for our blessed hope, the appearing of the glory of our great God and Savior Jesus Christ, who gave himself for us to redeem us from all lawlessness and to purify for himself a people for his own possession who are zealous for good works.

One could hardly find a more concise and comprehensive portrayal of the process of spiritual formation than the one Paul provides in v. 12: "training us to renounce ungodliness and worldly passions, and to live self-controlled, upright, and godly lives in the present age."

The "training" that grace provides (v. 12) consists of the present work of the Spirit in our churches and in our individual lives (the "already" aspect of eschatology, discussed above). Notice, however, that effectively appropriating God's sanctifying work in our lives demands a mindset focused upon (a) what God has done for us in history past (v. 14) and (b) what he has planned for history future (v. 13).

I recently read through Paul's letters to see how often he refers in some way to the return of Christ. I was astonished by the numbers of passages I found. In virtually every instance, moreover, Paul draws upon future hope in order to encourage his readers to remain faithful in the present. The following texts are representative. "Our blessed hope" (Titus 2:13) is intended to motivate us to

- refrain from judging others (Rom 2:5–16; 14:10–12; 1 Cor 4:5)
- endure suffering (Rom 8:18–25; 1 Thess 1:3; 2 Thess 1:5–11; 2 Tim 1:12; 2:12)
- resist immorality (Rom 13:11–14; Col 3:6; Titus 2:11–14)
- avoid divisions in the church (1 Cor 3:12–15)
- love one another (1 Cor 13:8–12; Col 1:4–5)
- proclaim the gospel (2 Cor 4:16—5:11; 1 Thess 2:19–20; 2 Tim 4:1)
- share generously with others (Gal 6:7–10)
- set our minds on things above (Phil 3:17–21; Col 3:3–4)
- act reasonably toward others (Phil 4:5)

- turn to God from idols (1 Thess 1:9–10)
- be encouraged and not grieve (1 Thess 4:13–18)
- remain alert (1 Thess 5:1–11)
- not be alarmed by current events (2 Thess 2:1–12)
- remain faithfully committed to the ministry (1 Tim 6:13–18)
- finish the race (2 Tim 4:8)

In the longest eschatological passage in his letters (1 Cor 15:12–57), Paul leverages the future resurrection of believers to challenge his readers concerning their lives in the here-and-now: "be steadfast, immovable, always abounding in the work of the Lord, knowing that in the Lord your labor is not in vain" (v. 58).

Paul clearly did not share our sense of disconnect between the present and the future. As Kyle Roberts puts it, "Biblical eschatology is neither escapist nor unconcerned with the present. Rather, God's plan for restoration gives history meaning. Eschatology is God's invitation to live in the kingdom in light of God's glorious future."[13]

The apostle John views the return of Christ as the prime motivator for the whole project of sanctification:

> When he appears we shall be like him, because we shall see him as he is. And everyone who thus hopes in him purifies himself as he is pure (1 John 3:2b–3).

The biblical witness is unequivocal. The "not yet" part of God's kingdom program is absolutely essential to faithfulness and progress in the Christian life. "Without hope we have nothing."[14]

Too Much Already

Today future eschatology is out of fashion. Few of us spend much time or energy consciously "waiting for our blessed hope" (Titus 2:13). Or teaching about it. The idea that God has something better in store for our future that might inspire us to live for him today—that "the sufferings of this present time are not worth comparing with the glory that is to be revealed to us"

---

13. Roberts, "Eschatology and Hope," 90.
14. Steele, *On the Way,* 133.

(Rom 8:18)—has become a hard sell in a culture that demands the immediate gratification of our every desire.

In 1990s, the seeker-sensitive movement focused almost exclusively on the here and now of daily Christian living. Today realized eschatology finds expression in an increasing concern for social justice among younger evangelicals. In many circles the "already" aspect of God's reign has virtually displaced future eschatology among those who are teaching and writing about the kingdom of God. Mark Saucy notes, "'Kingdom Now' rhetoric resounds everywhere, from Reformed theology, anxious to make good on the 'cultural mandate,' to the newly minted fellowships that are Emergent, missional, or simply emerging missional."[15] As a result, we preach and teach less and less in our churches about the second coming of Christ and the consummation of God's redemptive plan.

To be sure, there is something to be said for a realized eschatology. Kingdom now theology has encouraged evangelicals to care for unchurched people and cultural institutions in ways that we often did not in previous generations.

Thus OCF employs a full-time director for a mercy ministry that provides our people with a variety of opportunities to make a difference in their surrounding communities—painting schoolyards, tutoring inner-city children, welcoming foster children into our homes and homeless families into our church facility. No such ministry existed in the church where I served between 1975 and 1996. Provided that social justice does not displace the proclamation of the gospel as the central mission of the local church, this change should be warmly embraced.

The passages from Paul's letters demonstrate, however, that privileging the "already" aspect of God's kingdom to the near exclusion of what God has "not yet" brought to fruition, ultimately represents an unbiblical and unsustainable approach to Christian life and ministry. For according to the Scriptures cited above, it is precisely in our anticipation of what is yet to come that we find the spiritual resources necessary to live, grow, and make a difference in the lives of others in the here and now.

Most problematic for our spiritual pilgrimage is the tendency of kingdom now theology to be overly optimistic about God's work in our personal

---

15. Saucy, "*Regnum Spiriti*," 140–41. This is decidedly not the case among academic theologians, particularly in Germany. Pannenberg and Moltmann have both "sought to revitalize eschatology by demonstrating its forceful implications for the present" (Roberts, "Eschatology and Hope," 91). Burns refers to eschatology's "resurgence in academia" ("Hope: The Heart of Eschatology," 197).

lives in the present age.¹⁶ The potential result is a set of misplaced expectations and, finally, disappointment with God.

Living Unfulfilled

Do you ever wish that you could go back to the perfect shalom of the garden of Eden, where everything was exactly as God intends it to be? According to one wildly popular self-help guru, you can.

"You have everything you need for complete peace and total happiness right now." So claimed best-selling author Wayne W. Dyer, in a quote that is now plastered all over personal fulfillment websites.¹⁷

Dyer's assertion rings true to a degree. Problem people and problem circumstances do not need to define our lives. We do have all the necessary resources to find some peace and some happiness in the midst of life's challenges.

But not "*complete* peace and *total* happiness." Due to the fallen world in which we live, the full shalom for which Dyer longs will always elude us on this side of eternity. This is true for God's children as well. For not even a relationship with God can provide the ultimate shalom that we long for in the here and now.

The problem is not with God and his work in our lives. He has done his part. The problem is with us. On this side of eternity "we know only in part," as Paul puts it, "now we see in a mirror dimly" (1 Cor 13:9–12).

There is certainly peace to be had—enough of God's peace to enable us to deal with anything life throws at us (Phil 4:6–7, 13). But not perfect peace. Our sin-stained inability to fully appropriate and apprehend God's presence in our lives means that we will not in this life experience the "complete peace and total happiness" that Dyer writes about.

In a very real sense we must live our lives in a perpetual state of *un*fulfillment, in every area of our lives, until Jesus returns.¹⁸ This will

---

16. The debate continues concerning the degree to which God's reign is realized in the present age, and the implications of inaugurated eschatology for community activism and social justice. For two helpful discussions see Saucy, "*Regnum Spiriti*"; and Moore, "Till Every Foe Is Vanquished."

17. See, e.g., http://www.yourjoyologist.com/you-have-everything-you-need-for-complete-peace-and-total-happiness-right-now-wayne-w-dyer/.

http://www.braintrainingtools.org/skills/you-have-everything-you-need-for-complete-peace-and-total-happiness-right-now/.

18. I am indebted to Zachary Moore, my teaching assistant, for stimulating my

be the case both for the external circumstances of our lives and for our relationship with God.

A perpetual state of unfulfillment. It will do us well to stop and reflect for a moment on the phrase. The notion does not set well with the distorted emphasis on God's "already," so characteristic of the popular views of Christian spirituality that many of us have embraced.

American evangelicals will inevitably struggle with the idea that we are destined to remain unfulfilled in the here and now. The incessant narrative of personal fulfillment, which has defined secular culture for two generations, has convinced us otherwise.

Self-actualization. Self-esteem. Self-love. And self-fulfillment. We *can* be complete. We *can* be fulfilled. We *can* have it all. And we can have it all *now*. Or so we are told.

The culture's narrative has profoundly obscured a crucial biblical truth: on this side of eternity the world in which we live remains "in bondage to corruption" (Rom 8:21). The inevitable fallout for you and me will be a perpetual state of unfulfillment in every arena of life. This is simply part of what God's "not yet" is all about.

The Reality of a Creation in Bondage

As I indicated above, I am not advocating a world-denying withdrawal from culture. Works of social justice done in the name of Jesus can relieve suffering and bring much-deserved attention to the greatness of our God. Christians should do good for the world around us.

Neither am I suggesting that we cease to pray and to work toward physical health, relational wholeness, and vocational satisfaction in our own lives. Obedience to Scripture, fueled by the power of the Holy Spirit and the prayers of our brothers and sisters in Christ, often issues in change for the better in the quality of our individual lives.[19]

---

thinking along these lines.

19. Our focus in the chapter is future eschatology, but much more can be said on the positive side about God's work in the present age. One could hardly do better than to begin with Davis's treatment, *Meditation and Communion with God*. Davis purports to explore the implications of inaugurated eschatology for God's presence in the reading of Scripture, but the book accomplishes much more than this. Davis has gifted us with an inspiring, biblically robust exposition of the significance of God's "already" for life in the Spirit.

Many other times, however, our efforts do little or nothing to improve either our own circumstances or the general condition of our surrounding communities. This is most painfully apparent in our personal lives, where God faithfully walks us through the fires of trial and temptation but seldom extinguishes the fires themselves.

My wife and I spent last Saturday at a memorial service for Joann's forty-two-year-old cousin. Amy was a Christian who was full of life and in great health. Her sudden death—at the hands of a boyfriend who poisoned her and later died in a gun battle with local police—was a devastating shock to friends and family alike. Yesterday I was called to minister to a woman in our church whose sister lost a three-month-old baby boy.

Not only is our physical health and safety compromised by the brokenness of the fallen world in which we live. Also affected is the quality of relationships with friends and loved ones.

Even if we play our part well—and given our own pride and selfishness, we never finally do so—we cannot control the behavior of others. During the present era of salvation history, when God invites but does not enforce submission to his lordship, we will continue to be hurt and to be let down by others. We ourselves will hurt and let down others as well.

Life honestly embraced forces us to come to grips with biblical reality. The Scriptures consistently point to the future, not the present, as the time when "creation itself will be set free from its bondage to corruption and obtain the freedom of the glory of the children of God" (Rom 8:21).

Bondage is serious stuff. On this side of eternity God will not fully and finally fix the mess we have made of the life he has given us—whether in our personal lives or in the surrounding culture—with or without our help. To think otherwise is to set ourselves up for deep disappointment with God and thereby seriously to compromise the process of spiritual maturation.

Without a vital anticipation of "the appearing of the glory of our great God and Savior Jesus Christ" (Titus 2:13), the best we can do is to hope that God will set things straight in the here and now. In a world that is "groaning" in "bondage to corruption," such hope is decidedly misplaced.

Let us continue to pray and to work for God to have his way in our lives, in the lives of others, and in our surrounding communities. But let us also remain passionately consumed with an anticipation of that glorious day when "death shall be no more, neither shall there be mourning, nor crying, nor pain anymore, for the former things have passed away" (Rev 21:4).

Be Here Now

Ignoring or downplaying future eschatology is not only an unhealthy way to engage life's daily challenges. It is also theologically problematic. We gain a deeper appreciation for the significance of God's "not yet" in the biblical story line by noting the curious absence of future hope (a) in certain world religions and (b) in a dangerous heresy in the early Christian church.

It is hardly incidental that numbers of non-Christian religions lack a future eschatology. Back in the early 1970s, before my conversion, I spent a year dabbling in Taoism, Buddhism, and Hinduism. A musician friend gave me a copy of one of the most popular books on Eastern spirituality of the time. It was titled, *Be Here Now*, by Ram Dass (former Harvard psychiatrist Dr. Richard Alpert), affectionately known as the "Hippie bible."[20]

Be Here Now teaches that the secret to spirituality is to live wholly in the present by releasing all thoughts of past failure and future hope. God does not redeem our past. Neither does he offer hope for the future. There is no grand narrative of God working in history to fix the mess we have made of the life he has given us. No community-creating, world-redeeming story.

There is only the here and now. In the words of one enthusiastic reviewer of *Be Here Now*,

> The past is gone, an illusion which exerts all kinds of negative influences on the human psyche. The future is even more illusory, in that it is so transient. It could be years long, or it could be seconds—who knows? Life can only be truly experienced in the present—in the here and now—and if we are to find peace and spiritual freedom, we must first do away with our attachment to the past and the future.[21]

My girlfriend at the time became a disciple of a popular Eastern guru. He compelled her to destroy every photograph she possessed of previous events and relationships in order to free herself from the illusion of her past.[22]

---

20. Dass, *Be Here Now*.
21. Shankarji, "The Truth in Three Words."
22. Hinduism, Taoism, and Buddhism are much more complex and sophisticated than are our popular, Westernized amalgams of Eastern thought (e.g., *Be Here Now*). Nevertheless, they generally lack the kind of comprehensive, world-renewing eschatology that we encounter in the Judeo-Christian tradition. For an Asian perspective on eschatology, see Chia, *Hope for the World*.

This is all so very subtle and enticing precisely because it is partially true. Hurtful past experiences do exert "negative influences on the human psyche," as any rape victim will sadly attest. Worrying about a "transient" future can be emotionally paralyzing, as well.

The biblical alternative to past hurt and future uncertainty, however, is not to dismiss the past and future as illusory and to pretend that they do not exist. The Bible challenges us instead to situate our personal stories—past, present, and future—under the overarching rubric of God's great story of salvation, where God redeems past hurts and failures (Rom 8:28; Eph 1:7), in order to prepare us for a glorious future (Rom 8:18).

Neither the past nor the future is an illusion in the grand narrative of salvation history. As it turns out, remembering the past and anticipating the future are crucial for our spiritual development. We are to "proclaim the Lord's death" (past) "until he comes" (future) every time we celebrate the Lord's Supper in our churches (1 Cor 11:26).

Many of us need to read and reread John's vision of the future in Revelation 21–22, again and again, to remind ourselves that what Paul wrote in Rom 8:18 really is true: "the sufferings of this present time are not worth comparing with the glory that is to be revealed to us."

Being here now is good. For some of us, at any rate, particularly in the economically prosperous West.

Being there then will be unimaginably better. For all of us. Western evangelicals seem to have forgotten just how much better. And our forgetfulness in this regard has the potential to compromise the work of spiritual formation that God desires to accomplish in our lives and in our communities.

A Storyless Charade and the Gnostic Turn

Eschatology and story are, of course, closely connected, since for Christians the return of Christ marks the end of the biblical narrative and the beginning of the age to come. We saw in chapter 8 that a community depends upon the effectiveness of its defining narrative for group identity and social solidarity. Lose the story and you lose the community.

The same is true of the relationship between narrative and hope. Individual hope, like communal solidarity, depends upon story for its ongoing

Why We Need the Church to Become More Like Jesus

vitality. As Lanier Burns notes, "people find hope in cultural stories that give them personal meaning through collective purposes."[23]

Andrew Delbanco has recently traced what he calls the "diminution of hope" in recent American history directly to the loss of our cultural narrative.[24] Over the centuries America's story has gradually contracted so that our basis of hope has been transferred from God to nation to "the vanishing point of the self alone."[25]

Today all that is left is "instant gratification as the hallmark of the good life."[26] Lacking a robust cultural narrative, "possessive individualism tries to compensate with competitive self-display, but its storyless charade breaks down."[27] The result is "an ache for meaning that goes unrelieved."[28] Lose the story and you lose your hope.

The application to Christian formation should be patently clear. We cannot lose our story and still retain our hope. To lose the Christian story—especially the end of the story—is to open ourselves up to a loss of hope that renders America's "diminution of hope" utterly trivial and inconsequential by comparison. For the people of God, a "storyless charade" is simply not an option.

Lewis Smedes rightly insists that "there is nothing, repeat nothing, more critical for any one of us, young or old or anything in between, than the vitality of our hope."[29] And that hope must be based squarely on the "not yet" of God's redemptive plan. Lose our future hope, and all that remains is the limited purchase of a realized eschatology, which ultimately cashes out in discouragement and disappointment for all who unwittingly embrace it.

It is no accident that the first major heresy in Christian history—ancient Gnosticism—ignored biblical eschatology completely. Gnostics mined the Old and New Testaments for bits and pieces of data, but they left out the future-oriented story of redemption. God is not out at the end of history, promising to restore a broken people and a broken world. God

---

23. Burns, "Hope: The Heart of Eschatology," 192, describing the views of Delbanco, *Real American Dream*.

24. Delbanco, *Real American Dream*, 1.

25. Ibid., 103.

26. Ibid., 96–97.

27. Burns, "Hope: The Heart of Eschatology," 193.

28. Delbanco, *Real American Dream*, 107.

29. Smedes, *Standing on the Promises*, x.

Until Jesus Returns

is experienced in the here and now, when we become aware of a divine spark within us.

In view of what we have learned about the relationship between story and hope, what the gnostics did with Jesus was particularly insidious. Gnosticism took Jesus—and everything Jesus taught about his second coming—out of the story of Scripture and turned him into a purveyor of catchy one-liners.

Perhaps you are familiar with a document called the Gospel of Thomas. The one complete manuscript we possess was used by a group of gnostic Christians in Egypt around 350 CE. The Gospel of Thomas consists of a series of more than one hundred sayings of Jesus. Most are taken from Matthew, Mark, Luke, and John.

Unlike our four Gospels, however, the Gospel of Thomas contains no narrative. No story about Jesus. No Good Friday. No Easter Sunday. And no promise of Jesus's return. Eschatology—as we encounter it in Jesus's teachings and parables in the canonical Gospels (e.g., Matt 24–25)—is nowhere to be found in the Gospel of Thomas. And the author makes no attempt to fit Jesus into the Bible's overarching story of redemption. All that is left is just one pithy Jesus saying after another.

Taking Jesus out of the story (and the story out of Christianity) has been a primary threat to Christian orthodoxy for generations. There is a reason that the return of Christ has historically been a cardinal point of Christian doctrine. As we have seen above, and as the Bible unequivocally attests, a robust grasp of redemptive history—with its eschatological orientation—is absolutely essential for our spiritual formation as individual Christians.

Conclusion

Kingdom now theology works fine when things are going well in our lives. When life goes our way and we are basking in God's blessings in the here and now, we do not feel particularly compelled to think about the future.

But what about when things go bad? Unemployment. Divorce. Terminal cancer. The loss of a child. A world war. A holocaust. Thomas a Kempis wrote, "Jesus has many who love his kingdom of heaven, but few who bear his cross."[30]

---

30. Thomas à Kempis, *Imitation of Christ*, 2.11.

Why We Need the Church to Become More Like Jesus

The German theologian Jürgen Moltmann is arguably the greatest "future eschatologist" alive today. Moltmann did not always care about God's "not yet," or even about God, for that matter. He was sent to the front to fight for the Germans near the end of World War II. Moltmann surrendered to the Allies, and he became a Christian in a POW camp in Scotland shortly after the end of the war.

When Moltmann returned to his native Germany in 1948, he came face-to-face with what he describes as "concrete experiences of an overwhelming burden of guilt and of ghastly absurdity in my generation." It was a "condition of being unable to speak any longer of God, but all the while being compelled to speak of him."

"Of what else after all should one speak after Auschwitz," Moltmann exclaimed, "if not of God?!"[31]

The young German embarked on what would become an exceptionally illustrious career as a theologian. And his focus, because of—not in spite of—the horrors that surrounded him, was the "not yet" of God's plan of redemption. Moltmann's *Theology of Hope* became the most widely celebrated work on eschatology of the twentieth century. For Moltmann, "hope is nothing else than the expectation of those things which faith has believed to have been truly promised by God."[32]

While perhaps a bit overstated, Moltmann's comments about the place of God's "not yet" in Christian theology and praxis constitute a timely challenge to a generation of evangelicals who no longer have our eyes on the future: "The eschatological is not one element of Christianity, but it is the medium of Christianity as such, the key in which everything else is set, the glow that suffuses everything here in the dawn of an expected new day."[33]

> The one who testifies to these things says,
> "Surely I am coming soon"
> Amen. Come, Lord Jesus!
> (Rev 22:20)

---

31. Moltmann, "Autobiographical Note," 203–4. See also Moltmann, *Broad Place*.

32. Moltmann, *Theology of Hope*, 20.

33. Ibid., 16. Barth similarly opines, "Christianity that is not entirely and altogether eschatology has entirely and altogether nothing to do with Christ" (*Romans*, 314).

CONCLUSION

Why We Need the Church to Become More Like Jesus

Reflections about Community, Spiritual Formation, and the Story of Scripture

> "There is no such thing as 'Jesus and me.'"[1]
> —Peter Feldmeier

MORE THAN FORTY YEARS ago, Gordon Cosby wrote, "It is extremely rare to find a person who rejoices in his own uniqueness, who enjoys that bit of God's handiwork which is herself."[2]

We should call off the search.

A spiritual journey focused primarily upon my "uniqueness" as an individual will never produce the joyous person Cosby describes. For we were never meant to find ultimate joy in "that bit of God's handiwork which is [me]."

Not that we haven't tried. The path of American evangelicalism is littered with attempts to situate meaning and purpose in life almost exclusively in a "personal relationship with God." Meanwhile, we have been socialized by our culture to embrace a diluted and unbiblical view of Christian community. The result has been an unfortunate disconnect between the individual and the communal aspects of spiritual formation.

Many of us long to experience the fullness of God and his purpose for our lives. Not a whole lot of us ever do. One of the reasons, as we have seen,

---

1. Feldmeier, *Developing Christian*, 29.
2. Cosby, *Handbook for Mission Groups*, 98.

is that modern evangelicals have departed in some significant ways from the biblical view of life and growth that characterized early Christianity:

POPULAR EVANGELICAL SPIRITUALITY		
Me ---------------- *Experiencing God* --------- *In My Daily Life*		
INDIVIDUALISTIC	SUBJECTIVE	AHISTORICAL
EARLY CHRISTIAN SPIRITUALITY		
Us ---------------- *Making Disciples* -------- *Until Jesus Returns*		
COLLECTIVIST	OBJECTIVE	ESCHATOLOGICAL

The threefold contrast in the chart will serve as a useful map to retrace our steps through the material we covered in *Why We Need The Church to Become More Like Jesus*.

Me (Individualistic) versus Us (Collectivist)

The *Me* versus *Us* distinction is most basic. The contrast reflects a pair of very different and deeply rooted cultural values. It demanded more attention in the book than the other two comparative categories, because collectivist relational priorities are quite foreign to most of us.

Chapters 1 & 2

The ancient world was what social scientists call a strong-group culture, where the group took priority over the individual. The reverse is the case for most Euro-Western readers. For us the individual comes first.

Strong-group values not only characterized culture at-large in Mediterranean antiquity. We discovered that collectivist convictions also defined what it meant to be a Christian in the early church.

Jesus and the apostles affirmed the strong-group values of their surrounding culture by the very images they used to portray God's design for relationships in the local church. Chapter 1 unpacked the idea of strong-group community as expressed in the New Testament image of the church as the body of Christ. Chapter 2 then looked at the church as the family of God. Each of these metaphors portrays the church as markedly relational in orientation.

Conclusion: Why We Need the Church to Become More Like Jesus

Few of us today think of the church in such deeply relational terms. We have commodified what God intended to be communal. The church has become an institution with an increasing smorgasbord of options to help facilitate a personal relationship with God. We are the consumers.

The very fact that we ask one another, "How was church today?" tells us that we think of church not as a family gathering but rather as (1) a place to go with (2) programs to evaluate. We uncritically assume that the church is here primarily to help us as individuals to become more like Jesus.

The New Testament view of the church is quite the opposite. For Paul and the early Christians, we as individuals are here to help the church to grow into the kind of relational and missional community that God intends it to be. The church does not exist for me. Rather, I exist for the church and its mission.

We have seen what happens when we ignore this biblical priority and focus almost exclusively on the personal faith and spiritual pilgrimage of the individual. The American evangelical preoccupation with Jesus as personal savior has done little more than generate a utilitarian, consumerist approach to the Christian life that has drained the vitality out of our churches and left numbers of us deeply disappointed with our relationship with God.

This strong-group perspective does not negate the importance of growing in my personal relationship with God. Rather, it is an indispensable key to such growth. For, as we have seen throughout *Why We Need the Church to Become More Like Jesus,* I grow as an individual Christian to the degree that I am embedded in Christian community, enjoying intimate, life-giving relationships with others, and using my gifts to serve the church and the world.

Chapter 3

The Bible views strong-group community as the nonnegotiable setting for our growth as individual Christians. Yet we know all too well from our natural families that long-term intimate relationships can be life-giving or emotionally damaging. The same is true of our church families. It becomes crucial, in this regard, to make sure that we as individuals belong to a healthy church family with emotionally healthy leaders.

The ambiguity in the book's title is thus intentional. *We Need the Church.* But we also need *the Church to Become More* Like *Jesus.* The church

Why We Need the Church to Become More Like Jesus

is, after all, the body of Christ. In chapter 3, we outlined four characteristics of a healthy church and its organizational structure:

1. A Healthy Church Will Be Theologically Centered
2. A Healthy Church Will Be Sensitive to Process
3. A Healthy Church Will Be Open to Change
4. A Healthy Church Will Be Led by Pastors in Community

Chapter 4

This chapter came at the theme of spiritual formation in community from a different angle. Because ancient social values are so culturally foreign to us, the idea of the church as a family is often better caught than taught. Over the years, the Hellermans' church, OCF in El Segundo, California, has become a laboratory of sorts for the ideas you encountered in the first three chapters of the book. Chapter 4 contained several narratives penned by persons in our congregation to illustrate group-first Christianity in real life.

We also considered the ways community socialization contributes to our worldview as individuals. This is especially true for intergenerational relationships. By design, therefore, the stories in the chapter focused primarily upon the socializing function of relationships between persons at different life-stages in a local church family.

The genesis of Haven Academy of the Arts in a teenager's love for theater, of Eric and Jeannie Hardie's Sunday night community, the OCF wisdom council ministry—each of these in its own way testifies to the increasingly crucial role that intergenerational relationships are playing in our formation as individual Christians.

Chapter 5

We concluded our examination of the *Me* (individualistic) versus *Us* (collectivist) contrast on the chart with a look at recent trends in American evangelicalism. One of the first things students typically ask after coming to grips with the material in the first four chapters of this book, is, how did we depart so far from church as it appears in the New Testament?

The answer is quite simple. The biblical view of church has been hijacked and replaced by a view of the Christian life that owes more to

Conclusion: Why We Need the Church to Become More Like Jesus

American individualism and consumerism than it does to the teachings of Scripture. Chapter 5 traced three specific examples of this phenomenon: personal evangelism and *The Four Spiritual Laws* (1970s), the spiritual gifts craze (1980s), and the seeker-sensitive movement (1990s).

These trends reveal how susceptible American evangelicalism has been to the lure of Western individualism. The chapter concluded with a look at a more promising development, the spiritual formation movement (2000s), cautioning against indicators that this trend too could become caught in the trap of cultural compromise.

Experiencing God (Subjective) versus Making Disciples (Objective)

The next two chapters tackled a second contrast between popular evangelical spirituality and early Christian spirituality (see chart). Jesus did not leave *me* with a *great experience*. He left *us* with a *Great Commission*.

Actually, he left us with both. God has commissioned us to make disciples until Jesus returns. But he also wants us to experience his presence as individuals, in our daily lives.

The issue has to do with how we prioritize these two aspects of our faith, for they are not unrelated. As it turns out, we experience God in our daily lives to the degree that we are deeply rooted in a community that is sold out to reaching a broken world with the love of Jesus. Religious experience devoid of community and mission is a dead-end street.

The early Christians got this. They were all about the mission of God. We, by contrast, are often consumed with chasing after special, out-of-the ordinary experiences of God's presence.

Chapter 6

Here we considered what it means to experience God. I began by suggesting that much of our excessive longing for non-routine religious experience owes more the culture around us than to the teachings of Scripture. Experience has become the unfortunate—and ultimately unsatisfying—substitute for meaning and purpose in many areas of our lives.

Yet God very much desires for us to enjoy his presence in immediate and meaningful ways. It becomes important in this regard to distinguish between

1. ordinary manifestations of the indwelling Spirit in our daily lives (John 14:16–17, 23; Rom 8:9–17), and

2. extraordinary manifestations of the Spirit's power and other ecstatic experiences of God (Acts 4:31; 13:9; 2 Cor 12:1–4).

We discussed these two ways of experiencing God in some detail, concluding that Scripture challenges us to be sensitive to the ongoing promptings of the Holy Spirit in our walk with Christ. Pursuing intimacy with God is this sense is a biblical mandate.

In contrast, we do not see the early Christians individually pursuing non-routine, extraordinary experiences of God's presence. God certainly manifested himself in some remarkable ways in the early church. But in the New Testament, experiencing God's extraordinary presence is almost exclusively associated with engaging in God's mission, and with doing so in community with others.

This should not surprise us, since in his last instructions to his disciples, Jesus tied both (a) his ongoing presence ("I am with you always" [Matt 28:20]) and (b) the experience of the Holy Spirit's power ("you will receive power" [Acts 1:8]) to (c) the task of world evangelism. God's presence and God's power follow God's priorities.

In the final analysis, the relationship between *experiencing God* and *making disciples* runs in two directions. Most basically, a passion for the Great Commission should be the natural by-product of our ongoing relationship with the Holy Spirit (#1, above). The Spirit continually prompts us to live "giveaway lives" in the service of our fellow human beings, because of what God in Christ has done for us. "We love because he first loved us" (1 John 4:19).

As we respond to the Spirit and say (with the prophet Isaiah), "Here I am! Send me." (Isa 6:8), God occasionally—at times of his choosing—meets us in extraordinary ways to assist us in accomplishing his missional purposes (# 2, above). Like the early Christians in Jerusalem, we then become "filled with the Holy Spirit" so that we can "speak the word of God with boldness" (Acts 4:31).

Chapter 7

We focused in this chapter on the mission of the people of God, drawing primarily from 1 Pet 2, where Peter identifies Christians as a royal priesthood,

Conclusion: Why We Need the Church to Become More Like Jesus

commissioned to (1) "offer spiritual sacrifices acceptable to God" and (2) "proclaim the excellencies of him who called you out of darkness into his marvelous light" (1 Pet 2:5, 9).

As has been the case throughout the book, the topic of community—the overarching theme of *Why We Need the Church to Become More Like Jesus*—surfaced in our discussion of mission as well. Jesus does not intend for us to engage in his disciple making mandate (Matt 28:18–20) alone, relationally isolated from others in our church family. Ministry is meant to be done in community with others.

We encountered some troubling data about the current emotional and spiritual health of friendless pastors and their families. Ministerial burnout has become all too common among both vocational and volunteer leaders in our churches. We noted, in contrast, that the apostle Paul appears to have enjoyed robust emotional and spiritual health throughout a lengthy missionary career marked at nearly every turn by serious people problems.

I suggested that a key to Paul's staying power in ministry was the relationships he shared with his fellow missionaries and church leaders. A careful examination of the New Testament data thoroughly deconstructs the popular view of Paul as a superapostle who accomplished great things singlehandedly, without the help of others. Rather, both Acts and the epistles portray Paul consistently serving in community with various co-workers with whom he was deeply connected.

God intends for us to find purpose in life by joyfully and sacrificially embracing the most honorable and meaningful task imaginable: bringing God to a hurting world, and bringing a hurting world to God. But we are to engage in this life-consuming mission together, in community with our brothers and sisters in Christ.

In My Daily Life (Ahistorical) versus Until Jesus Returns (Eschatological)

The last two chapters compared the future orientation of early Christianity with today's tendency to emphasize God's present activity in our individual lives. The contrast appears on the chart in the phrases *In My Daily Life* (popular evangelical spirituality) versus *Until Jesus Returns* (early Christian spirituality).

We came at the distinction in two ways. Chapter 8 highlighted the function of the biblical narrative in our lives as Christians. Chapter 9 focused more specifically upon the end of God's story, the return of Christ.

Chapter 8

Story is a trendy thing in our postmodern world. And rightly so where spiritual growth is concerned. Embracing God's story—and getting our place in it right—is indispensable to being conformed to the image of Christ.

Social scientists have spent much energy in recent years studying the propensity of human beings to generate narratives that pull together and explain the otherwise random data we encounter along life's way. I am not referring just to people who write for a living. We all tell stories. Humans are "Storytelling Animals."[3]

This is especially the case for groups of people. Nearly every people group throughout world history has had a unifying narrative that provides the group with (a) a sense of social identity in relation to the outside world and (b) relational solidarity among group members themselves. People who rally around the truth of a compelling story about their group's origins and destiny—and who faithfully pass on that story to future generations—tend to thrive as a vibrant and enduring community.

People groups that fail to retain their story experience a loss of identity and, ultimately, social fragmentation. As the story is lost, younger members no longer view themselves as important actors in a dynamic and defining group narrative.

Lose the story and you lose the community.

The implications for our spiritual lives and for the local church are manifold. At the very least, we ought be deeply concerned about the lack of biblical literacy in our congregations. Many Christians today cannot even tell God's story, let alone understand and articulate their role in the magnificent narrative of creation, fall, redemption, and restoration that we call the Bible.

Topical teaching addressed solely to felt needs is partly to blame (see chapter 5, on the seeker-sensitive movement). Precisely because the approach pays little attention to the overarching narrative of Scripture, we fail to grasp the part we are to play in God's great story. The inevitable result

---

3. The title of a book by Jonathan Gottschall.

Conclusion: Why We Need the Church to Become More Like Jesus

is that communal identity and relational solidarity suffer, and the church becomes little more than a self-help station for individual believers.

We can also have a story but have the wrong one. Millions of us have bought into the idea (popularized by a well-intended gospel tract) that "God has a wonderful plan for your life."

When we turn to Scripture, however, we discover that God and his "wonderful plan" are much bigger than the constrained horizons of me and my daily life. Indeed, my spiritual pilgrimage is but one of millions of brief footnotes to God's great story of redemption. An important footnote, to be sure. But a footnote nonetheless.

God's story encompasses the whole universe. It involves creation, fall, redemption, and restoration. The story runs from the first chapter of Genesis to the end of Revelation. And God's wonderful plan for my life is for me to play my part in his story.

Constant exposure to the biblical narrative reinforces this paradigm. For as we immerse ourselves in the story of Scripture, "we are," in the words of Dietrich Bonhoeffer, "torn out of our own existence and set down in the midst of the holy history of God on earth."[4]

Chapter 9

The final chapter brought us, appropriately enough, to the theme of eschatology. Here we arrive at the place in God's grand narrative where Jesus returns to fix the mess we've made of the life he has given us, the moment when "the creation itself will be set free from its bondage to corruption and obtain the freedom of the glory of the children of God" (Rom 8:21).

When we retell God's story at the Lord's Table, we are to "proclaim the Lord's death *until he comes*." (1 Cor 11:26). Unfortunately, eschatology gets little attention today in church teaching, or in current thinking about spiritual formation. As the chart indicates, we have traded in *Until Jesus Returns* for *In My Daily Life*. Instead of eagerly anticipating "the appearing of the glory of our great God and Savior Jesus Christ"—what the Bible calls "our blessed hope" (Titus 2:13), we set our sights on the hope that God will somehow make life more manageable on this side of eternity.

At one level this is rather odd since according to the Bible a fervent eschatological outlook is indispensable for abundant Christian living in the here-and-now. When, in contrast, we prioritize the present, and ignore the

---

4. Bonhoeffer, *Life Together*, 53.

Why We Need the Church to Become More Like Jesus

future, we deprive ourselves of the benefits of both. For we expect too much of God on this side of eternity, and not enough of him for the future.

Current imbalance between the already versus the not yet of God's eschatological program has left numbers of Christians expecting God to act in ways he never promised to act. Little wonder that so many of us are disappointed with our spiritual lives.

In the final analysis, there is no Story without the end of the Story. As Paul put it in the longest discussion in his letters about the return of Christ, "If in Christ we have hope in this life only, we are of all people most to be pitied" (1 Cor 15:19).

Recapturing in our congregations a biblical emphasis on the return of Jesus will contribute greatly toward our growth as individual Christians and the health of our churches. Only a vibrant future hope can effectively motivate us to remain faithful to God in the here-and-now, that is, to "be steadfast, immovable, always abounding in the work of the Lord, knowing that in the Lord your labor is not in vain" (1 Cor 15:58).

Conclusion

Christian community. The Great Commission. Future hope. It all sounds a bit old-fashioned. Not very trendy. Yet these three aspects of the faith continue to define our place in the world as Christians. And they provide the essential context for individual progress in the Christian life.

Three closing observations are in order regarding the contrast reflected in the chart:

POPULAR EVANGELICAL SPIRITUALITY		
Me --------------- *Experiencing God* --------- *In My Daily Life*		
INDIVIDUALISTIC	SUBJECTIVE	AHISTORICAL
EARLY CHRISTIAN SPIRITUALITY		
Us ---------------- *Making Disciples* -------- *Until Jesus Returns*		
COLLECTIVIST	OBJECTIVE	ESCHATOLOGICAL

First, striking a balance will be challenging, because we are all wired differently. Some of us are doers. Others are thinkers. Some readers will be gregarious extroverts. Others are reserved introverts.

Conclusion: Why We Need the Church to Become More Like Jesus

We all tend to gravitate toward those aspects of the Christian life that happen to fit our temperaments. This means that each of us will need to exercise a degree of intentionality to pursue all three characteristics of early Christian spirituality for healthy spiritual life and growth.

Consider the alternatives. We can be sold out to Jesus's disciple-making mission, anxiously awaiting the return of Christ, and still set ourselves up for discouragement and burnout if we fail to embrace the values and practices of strong-group, New Testament community.

The other two aspects of early Christian spirituality are similarly indispensable. Substitute *experiencing God* for *making disciples*, and we lose our purpose for living, even if we become deeply rooted in a relational community with a sound eschatological perspective. Devalue the grand narrative of Scripture—with its life-giving promise of the future restoration of all creation—and we risk losing our communal identity and open ourselves up to an overly realized eschatology that results in disappointment with God's work in our lives.

It is not a matter of getting it right in one or two areas. The way of life reflected in early Christian spirituality is holistic. We are to make disciples until Jesus returns deeply rooted in a vibrant local church family.

Second, I want us to consider how the two perspectives on Christian spirituality surveyed above cash out in terms of our personal lives and the mission of our churches. We can complete the chart as follows:

POPULAR EVANGELICAL SPIRITUALITY		
Me --------------- *Experiencing God* --------- *In My Daily Life*		
INDIVIDUALISTIC	SUBJECTIVE	AHISTORICAL
ASKS: *What can* ***GOD*** *do for* ***ME?***		
PRODUCES: *A **PERSON** with an **EXPERIENCE***		
EARLY CHRISTIAN SPIRITUALITY		
Us --------------- *Making Disciples* -------- *Until Jesus Returns*		
COLLECTIVIST	OBJECTIVE	ESCHATOLOGICAL
ASKS: *What can* ***WE*** *do for* ***GOD?***		
PRODUCES: *A **COMMUNITY** with a **MISSION***		

The approach reflected in popular evangelical spirituality, preoccupied as it is with personal experience in the here and now, inevitably asks the question, what can *God* to do for *me*? The most we can hope for by way of result, is, make me a *person* with an *experience*.

Why We Need the Church to Become More Like Jesus

Early Christian spirituality, precisely because of its collectivist missional and eschatological worldview, encourages us to ask instead, what can *we* do for *God*? Such an outlook more naturally generates a *community* with a *mission*—the New Testament model for a local church.

Finally, I want to respond to a challenge I get nearly every time I teach through the material in *Why We Need the Church to Become More Like Jesus*, especially when I roll out the above chart, with its sharp contrast between popular evangelical spirituality and early Christian spirituality. The push-back goes something like this:

> Joe, doesn't God want us to individually experience his presence and power in our daily lives *and* to partner with our fellow believers to make disciples until Jesus returns? Aren't both biblical? Haven't you set up a false dichotomy between the two approaches?

My answer is an unqualified yes on all three counts. I have purposely set up what is ultimately an untenable contrast in the chart as a heuristic device in order to help us see just how out of balance we have become.

The issue, in the final analysis, is one of priorities, a cart-before-the-horse scenario (to adopt a well-worn image). Pursuing God alone, apart from the local church and its mission, is a dead-end street that will never ultimately satisfy. We experience the presence and power of God in our daily lives as individuals when we are relationally rooted in a local church community that is sold out to bringing the love of Jesus to a broken world and to bringing broken people to the cross. This is the message of *Why We Need the Church to Become More Like Jesus*.

A silly little tale about a tail will help drive this truth home.

Once upon a time, as the story goes, a little kitten was running round and round in circles, chasing its tail. The kitten had discovered that happiness was in his tail, and he was determined to get ahold of it. In spite of his best efforts, however, the little fellow could never move fast enough to get his mouth around that tail in order to hang on to it for any length of time. Happiness, it seemed, was ever elusive.

Before too long, an older, wiser feline approached the kitten, now nearly exhausted from his frantic pursuit. "Hear the wisdom of the aged, little one," she proclaimed. "I too discovered when I was a kitten that happiness is in my tail. But, just like you, try as I might, I could never take hold of it. Soon, however, I had an astounding, life-changing revelation. Whenever I stop chasing my tail and go about my business, my tail follows me wherever I go."

Conclusion: Why We Need the Church to Become More Like Jesus

Making disciples until Jesus returns is our business on this side of eternity. Take the challenge. Give yourself away to a healthy Christian community that is playing its part in God's great story of redemption. Like so many others throughout the history of the Christian church, you will discover that the presence of God and the joy of the Lord follow you wherever you go.

Bibliography

Allen, Holly Catterton, and Christine Lawton Ross. *Intergenerational Christian Formation: Bringing the Whole Church Together in Ministry, Community, and Worship.* Downers Grove, IL: IVP Academic, 2012.
Anderson, Keith R., and Randy D. Reese. *Spiritual Mentoring: A Guide for Seeking and Giving Direction.* Downers Grove, IL: InterVarsity, 1999.
Anizor, Uche, and Hank Voss. *Representing Christ: A Vision for the Priesthood of All Believers.* Downers Grove, IL: IVP Academic, 2016.
Armstrong, Chris. "The Rise, Frustration, and Revival of Evangelical Spiritual Ressourcement." *Journal of Spiritual Formation & Soul Care* 2/1 (2009) 113–21.
Arnold, Clinton E. *Ephesians.* Zondervan Exegetical Commentary on the New Testament. Grand Rapids: Zondervan, 2010.
Barth, Karl. *Epistle to the Romans.* Translated by Edwyn C. Hoskyn. London: Oxford University Press, 1933.
Bauckham, Richard. *Bible and Mission: Christian Witness in a Postmodern World.* Grand Rapids: Baker Academic, 2004.
Beale, Gregory K. "The Eschatological Conception of New Testament Theology." In *Eschatology in the Bible and Theology,* edited by Kent E. Brower and Mark W. Elliott, 11–52. Downers Grove, IL: InterVarsity, 1997.
Bellah, Robert N., et al. *Habits of the Heart: Individualism and Commitment in American Life.* Berkeley: University of California Press, 1985.
Benner, David G. *Spirituality and the Awakening Self: The Sacred Journey of Transformation.* Grand Rapids: Brazos, 2012.
Berding, Kenneth. *Bible Revival: Recommitting Ourselves to One Book.* Wooster, OH: Weaver, 2014.
Berger, Peter L. *A Rumor of Angels: Modern Society and the Rediscovery of the Supernatural.* Anchor Books. New York: Doubleday, 1970.
Berger, Peter L., and Thomas Luckmann. *The Social Construction of Reality: A Treatise in the Sociology of Knowledge.* Garden City, NY: Anchor, 1967.
Blackaby, Henry T., et al. *Experiencing God: Knowing and Doing the Will of God.* Rev. and exp. ed. Nashville: Broadman & Holman, 2004.
Boa, Kenneth. *Conformed to His Image: Biblical and Practical Approaches to Spiritual Formation.* Grand Rapids: Zondervan, 2001.
Bock, Darrell L. "New Testament Community and Spiritual Formation." In *Foundations of Spiritual Formation: A Community Approach to Becoming Like Christ,* edited by Paul Pettit, 103–19. Grand Rapids: Kregel, 2008.

Bibliography

Bonhoeffer, Dietrich. *Life Together*. Translated and with an introduction by John Doberstein. New York: Harper, 1954.

Brown, Jeannine K., et al. *Becoming Whole and Holy: An Integrative Conversation about Spiritual Formation*. Grand Rapids: Brazos, 2011.

Buckley, Francis J., and Donald B. Sharp. *Deepening Christian Life: Integrating Faith and Maturity*. San Francisco: Harper & Row, 1987.

Burns, J. Lanier. "Hope: The Heart of Eschatology." In *Looking into the Future: Evangelical Studies in Eschatology*, edited by David W. Baker, 177–98. ETS Study Series. Grand Rapids: Baker Academic, 2001.

Carlson, Kent, and Mike Lueken. *Renovation of the Church: What Happens When a Seeker Church Discovers Spiritual Formation*. Downers Grove, IL: IVP Academic, 2011.

Carson, D. A. *Becoming Conversant with the Emerging Church*. Grand Rapids: Zondervan, 2005.

———. *The Gospel according to John*. Pillar New Testament Commentary. Grand Rapids: Eerdmans, 1991.

Chandler, Diane J. *Christian Spiritual Formation: An Integrated Approach for Personal and Relational Wholeness*. Downers Grove, IL: IVP Academic, 2014.

Charles, J. D. "Vice and Virtue Lists." In *Dictionary of New Testament Background*, edited by Craig A. Evans and Stanley E. Porter, 1252–57. Downers Grove, IL: InterVarsity, 2000.

Chia, Roland. *Hope for the World: A Christian Vision of Last Things*. Downers Grove, IL: IVP Academic, 2006.

Coe, John H. "Musings on the Dark Night of the Soul: Insights from St. John of the Cross on Developmental Spirituality." *Journal of Psychology and Theology* 28/4 (2000) 293–307.

Copan, Victor A. *Saint Paul as Spiritual Director: An Analysis of the Imitation of Paul with Implications and Applications to the Practice of Spiritual Direction*. Eugene, OR: Wipf & Stock, 2008.

———. "Spiritual Formation and St. Paul as Spiritual Director: Determining His Primary Aims." *Journal of Spiritual Formation & Soul Care* 3/2 (2010) 140–54.

Cosby, Gordon. *Handbook for Mission Groups*. Waco, TX: Word, 1975.

Crabb, Lawrence J., Jr. *Basic Principles of Biblical Counseling*. Grand Rapids: Zondervan, 1975.

Davis, John Jefferson. *Meditation and Communion with God: Contemplating Scripture in an Age of Distraction*. Downers Grove, IL: IVP Academic, 2012.

Dass, Ram. *Be Here Now*. Questa, NM: Lama Foundation, 1971.

Delbanco, Andrew. *The Real American Dream: A Meditation on Hope*. The William E. Massey, Sr. Lectures in the History of American Civilization 1998. Cambridge: Harvard University Press, 2000.

Diaz, Naelys, et al. "Attachment Style, Spirituality, and Depressive Symptoms among Individuals in Substance Abuse Treatment." *Journal of Social Service Research* 40/3 (2014) 313–24.

Dykstra, Craig R. *Vision and Character: A Christian Educator's Alternative to Kohlberg*. 1981. Reprint, Eugene, OR: Wipf & Stock, 2008.

Erickson, Erik. H. *Identity and the Life Cycle: Selected Papers*. New York: Norton, 1980.

Feldmeier, Peter. *The Developing Christian: Spiritual Growth through the Life Cycle*. Mahwah, NJ: Paulist, 2007.

Bibliography

Foster, Richard J. *Celebration of Discipline: The Path to Spiritual Growth*. 25th anniversary ed. San Francisco: HarperSanFrancisco, 1998.

Freisen, Garry, with J. Robin Maxson. *Decision Making and the Will of God: A Biblical Alternative to the Traditional View*. 25th anniversary ed. Revised and updated. Sisters, OR: Multnomah Books, 2004.

Gottschall, Jonathan. *The Storytelling Animal: How Stories Make Us Human*. Boston: Mariner Books, 2010.

Grenz, Stanley J. *The Social God and the Relational Self: A Trinitarian Theology of the Imago Dei*. The Matrix of Christian Theology. Louisville: Westminster John Knox, 2001.

———. *Theology for the Community of God*. 7th ed. Grand Rapids: Eerdmans, 2000.

Gurr, Ted Robert, and Barbara Harff. *Ethnic Conflict in World Politics*. Dilemmas in World Politics. Boulder, CO: Westview, 1994.

Haas, Gunther. "The Significance of Eschatology for Christian Ethics." In *Looking into the Future: Evangelical Studies in Eschatology*, edited by David W. Baker, 325–41. ETS Study Series. Grand Rapids: Baker Academic, 2001.

Harff, Barbara, and Ted Robert Gurr. *Ethnic Conflict in World Politics*. Dilemmas in World Politics. 2nd ed. Boulder, CO: Westview, 2004.

Hawkins, Greg L., and Cally Parkinson. *Reveal: Where Are You?* Barrington, IL: Willow Creek Resources, 2007.

Hendricks, Howard. Foreword to *Foundations of Spiritual Formation: A Community Approach to Becoming Like Christ*, edited by Paul Pettit, 9–14. Grand Rapids: Kregel, 2008.

Hellerman, Joseph H. *The Ancient Church as Family*. Minneapolis: Fortress, 2001.

———. *Embracing Shared Ministry: Power and Status in the Early Church and Why It Matters Today*. Grand Rapids: Kregel, 2013.

———. *Jesus and the People of God: Reconfiguring Ethnic Identity*. New Testament Monographs 21. Sheffield: Sheffield Phoenix, 2007.

———. *When the Church Was a Family*. Nashville: B&H, 2009.

Hjelm, Titus. *Social Constructionisms: Approaches to the Study of the Human World*. Basingstoke, UK: Palgrave MacMillan, 2014.

Howard, Evan B. *The Brazos Introduction to Christian Spirituality*. Grand Rapids: Brazos, 2008.

Iacoboni, Marco. *Mirroring People: The New Science of How We Connect with Others*. New York: Farrar, Straus & Giroux, 2008.

Issler, Klaus D. "The Soul and Spiritual Formation." In *Foundations of Spiritual Formation: A Community Approach to Becoming Like Christ*, edited by Paul Pettit, 121–42. Grand Rapids: Kregel, 2008.

Johnston, Gordon. "Old Testament Community and Spiritual Formation." In *Foundations of Spiritual Formation: A Community Approach to Becoming Like Christ*, edited by Paul Pettit, 71–101. Grand Rapids: Kregel, 2008.

Kegan, Robert. *The Evolving Self: Problem and Process in Human Development*. Cambridge: Harvard University Press, 1982.

Keller, Timothy. *Center Church: Doing Balanced, Gospel-Centered Ministry in Your City*. Grand Rapids: Zondervan, 2012.

Langer, Rick. "Points of Unease with the Spiritual Formation Movement." *Journal of Spiritual Formation & Soul Care* 5/2 (2012) 182–206.

Lewis, Gordon R. *Decide for Yourself: A Theological Workbook*. Downers Grove, IL: InterVarsity, 1970.

Bibliography

Lincoln, Andrew T. *Ephesians*. Word Biblical Commentary 42. Nashville: Nelson, 2014.

Loewen, James W. *Lies My Teacher Told Me: Everything Your American History Textbook Got Wrong*. New York: Touchstone, 1996.

London, H. B., Jr., and Neil B. Wiseman. *Pastors at Greater Risk*. Ventura, CA: Gospel Light, 2003.

Malina, Bruce J. *Christian Origins and Cultural Anthropology: Practical Models for Biblical Interpretation*. 1986. Reprint, Eugene, OR: Wipf & Stock, 2010.

McLaren, Brian D. *The Church on the Other Side: Doing Ministry in the Postmodern Matrix*. Grand Rapids: Zondervan, 2003.

Merton, Thomas. *No Man Is an Island*. Boston: Shambala, 2005.

Moltmann, Jürgen. *Theology of Hope: On the Ground and the Implications of a Christian Eschatology*. Translated by James W. Leitch. Twentieth Century Religious Thought. Minneapolis: Fortress, 1993.

Moore, Russell D. "Till Every Foe Is Vanquished." In *Looking into the Future: Evangelical Studies in Eschatology*, edited by David W. Baker, 342–61. ETS Study Series. Grand Rapids: Baker Academic, 2001.

Morris, Colin. *The Discovery of the Individual: 1050–1200*. Medieval Academy Reprints for Teaching 19. Toronto: University of Toronto Press, 1987.

Morrow, Jonathan. "Introducing Spiritual Formation." In *Foundations of Spiritual Formation: A Community Approach to Becoming Like Christ*, edited by Paul Pettit, 37–41. Grand Rapids: Kregel, 2008.

Mulholland, M. Robert, Jr. *Shaped by the Word: The Power of Scripture in Spiritual Formation*. Nashville: Upper Room Books, 2000.

———. "Spirituality and Transformation." In *Dictionary of Christian Spirituality*, edited by Glen G. Scorgie et al., 216–21. Grand Rapids: Zondervan, 2011.

Nelson, John E., and Richard N. Bolles. *What Color Is Your Parachute? For Retirement: Planning a Prosperous, Healthy, and Happy Future*. 2nd ed. Berkeley: Ten Speed, 2010.

Nelson, Peter K. *Spiritual Formation: Ever Forming, Never Formed*. Downers Grove, IL: InterVarsity, 2010.

Nienhuis, David R. "The Problem of Evangelical Biblical Illiteracy: A View from the Classroom." *Modern Reformation* 19/1 (2010) 10–13, 17.

Nisbett, Richard E. *The Geography of Thought: How Asians and Westerners Think Differently—and Why*. New York: Free Press, 2003.

Ollrog, W.-H. "Sunergos." In *Exegetical Dictionary of the New Testament*, edited by Horst Balz and Gerhard Schneider, 3:303. 3 vols. Grand Rapids: Eerdmans, 1993.

Packer, J. I. *Keep in Step with the Spirit*. Old Tappan, NJ: Revell, 1984.

Parks, Sharon. "Love Tenderly." In *To Act Justly, Love Tenderly, Walk Humbly*, edited by Walter Brueggemann, et al., 29–43. 1986. Eugene, OR: Wipf & Stock, 1997.

Patterson, O. "Context and Choice in Ethnic Allegiance: A Theoretical Framework and Caribbean Case Study." In *Ethnicity: Theory and Experience*, edited by Nathan Glazer and Daniel P. Moynihan, 305–49. Cambridge: Harvard University Press, 1975.

Pettit, Paul. "Introduction." In *Foundations of Spiritual Formation: A Community Approach to Becoming Like Christ*, edited by Paul Pettit, 17–26. Grand Rapids: Kregel, 2008.

———, ed. *Foundations of Spiritual Formation: A Community Approach to Becoming Like Christ*. Grand Rapids: Kregel, 2008.

Porter, Steve L. "Sanctification in a New Key: Relieving Evangelical Anxieties over Spiritual Formation." *Journal of Spiritual Formation & Soul Care* 1/2 (2008) 144–47.

Bibliography

Prager, Dennis. *Still the Best Hope: Why the World Needs American Values to Triumph.* New York: Broadside, 2012.

Putnam, Robert D. *Bowling Alone: The Collapse and Revival of American Community.* New York: Simon & Schuster, 2000.

Reed, Angela H. *Quest for Spiritual Community: Reclaiming Spiritual Guidance for Contemporary Congregations.* London: T. & T. Clark, 2011.

Roberts, Kyle A. "Eschatology and Hope." In *Dictionary of Christian Spirituality*, edited by Glen G. Scorgie et al., 89–94. Grand Rapids: Zondervan, 2011.

Rolheiser, Roland. *The Shattered Lantern: Rediscovering the Felt Presence of God.* London: Hodder & Stoughton, 1994.

Russell, Walt. *Playing with Fire: How the Bible Ignites Change in Your Soul.* Colorado Springs, CO: NavPress, 2000.

Saucy, Mark. "*Regnum Spiriti*: The Kingdom of God and Spiritual Formation." *Journal of Spiritual Formation & Soul Care* 4/2 (2011) 140–54.

Scazzero, Peter, and Warren Bird. *The Emotionally Healthy Church: A Strategy for Discipleship That Actually Changes Lives.* Grand Rapids; Zondervan, 2003.

Seidel, Andrew. "Leadership and Spiritual Formation." In *Foundations of Spiritual Formation: A Community Approach to Becoming Like Christ*, edited by Paul Pettit, 177–94. Grand Rapids: Kregel, 2008.

Schaller, Lyle E. *The Very Large Church: New Rules for Leaders.* Nashville: Abingdon, 2000.

Smedes, Lewis. *Standing on the Promises.* Nashville: Nelson, 1998.

Smith, Christian, et al. *American Evangelicalism: Embattled and Thriving.* Chicago: University of Chicago Press, 1998.

Steele, Les L. *On the Way: A Practical Theology of Christian Formation.* 1990. Reprint, Eugene, OR: Wipf & Stock, 1998.

Steere, Douglas V. *Gleanings: A Random Harvest.* Nashville: Upper Room, 1986.

Thiselton, Anthony C. "Signs of the Times." In *The Future as God's Gift: Explorations in Christian Eschatology*, edited by David Fergusson and Marcel Sarot, 9–39. T. & T. Clark Academic Paperbacks. Explorations in Contemporary Theology. Edinburgh: T. & T. Clark, 2000.

Thomas à Kempis. *The Imitation of Christ.* Translated by Leo Sherley-Price. London: Penguin, 1952.

Thompson, Curt. *Anatomy of the Soul: Surprising Connections between Neuroscience and Spiritual Practices That Can Transform Your Life and Relationships.* Carol Stream, IL: Tyndale House, 2012.

Veith, Gene Edward, Jr. *God at Work: Your Christian Vocation in All of Life.* Focal Point Series. Wheaton, IL: Crossway, 2002.

Wallace, Daniel B. *Greek Grammar beyond the Basics.* Grand Rapids: Zondervan, 1996.

Whitney, Donald S. *Spiritual Disciplines within the Church: Participating Fully in the Body of Christ.* Chicago: Moody, 1996.

Wiesel, Elie. *The Gates of the Forest.* Translated by Frances Frenaye. New York: Holt, Rinehart & Winston, 1966.

Wilhoit, James C. *Spiritual Formation as if the Church Mattered: Growing in Christ through Community.* Grand Rapids: Baker Academic, 2008.

Willard, Dallas. *Hearing God: Developing a Conversational Relationship with God.* Updated and expanded ed. Downers Grove, IL: IVP Books, 2012.

———. *The Spirit of the Disciplines: Understanding How God Changes Lives.* 2nd ed. San Francisco: Harper & Row, 1999.

Bibliography

Yankelovich, Daniel. "Trends in American Cultural Values." *Criterion* 35/3 (1996) 2–9.

Yep, Jeanette, et al. *Following Jesus without Dishonoring Your Parents: Asian American Discipleship*. Downers Grove, IL: InterVarsity, 1998.

Zinn, Howard. *A People's History of the United States*. New York: Harper Perennial Modern Classics, 2005.

Websites

The Barna Group. "5 Reasons Millennials Stay Connected to the Church." September 17, 2013. Research Releases in Generations and Millennials. https://www.barna.org/barna-update/millennials/635-5-reasons-millennials-stay-connected-to-church#.U9LKE4BpV7U/.

———. "New Research on the State of Discipleship." Research Releases in Leaders & Pastors. December 1, 2015. https://www.barna.com/research/new-research-on-the-state-of-discipleship/.

———. "The State of the Bible 2013." American Bible Society. http://www.americanbible.org/uploads/content/State%20of%20the%20Bible%20Report%202013.pdf/.

Bloom, Linda, and Charlie Bloom. "The Surprising Secret to Health and Longevity." *Psychology Today*, April 3, 2013. https://www.psychologytoday.com/blog/stronger-the-broken-places/201304/the-surprising-secret-health-and-longevity/.

Bright, Bill. *The Four Spiritual Laws*. CruStore.org. http://crustore.org/downloads/4laws.pdf/.

Carnell, Susan. "Bad Boys, Bad Brains." *Psychology Today*, May 14, 2012. http://www.psychologytoday.com/blog/bad-appetite/201205/bad-boys-bad-brains/.

Demore, Timothy. "Man, Movement, Machine, Monument." *The Blog Standard*, September 9, 2012. https://tpdemore.blogspot.com/2012/09/man-movement-machine-monument.html/.

Dyer, Wayne W. Brain Quotes. http://www.braintrainingtools.org/skills/you-have-everything-you-need-for-complete-peace-and-total-happiness-right-now/.

———. *Your Joyologist*. Website. http://www.yourjoyologist.com/you-have-everything-you-need-for-complete-peace-and-total-happiness-right-now-wayne-w-dyer/.

Eckholm, Erik. "Unmarried Pastor, Seeking a Job, Sees Bias." *New York Times*, March 21, 2011. http://www.nytimes.com/2011/03/22/us/22pastor.html?pagewanted=all&_r=0/.

Hellerman, Joseph. "Our Priorities Are Off When Family Is More Important Than Church." *Christianity Today*, August 4, 2016. http://www.christianitytoday.com/ct/2016/august-web-only/if-our-families-are-more-important-than-our-churches-we-nee.html?start=1/.

Lukasik, Dan. "Is Lack of Life Meaning Your Depression Trigger?" *Lawyers with Depression*, December 15, 2010. http://www.lawyerswithdepression.com/articles/is-lack-of-life-meaning-your-depression-trigger/.

Ohmer, John. "Man, Movement, Machine, Monument." *Episcopal Café*, October 6, 2012. http://www.episcopalcafe.com/man_movement_machine_monument/.

PastorBurnout.com. "Pastor Burnout Statistics." http://www.pastorburnout.com/pastor-burnout-statistics.html/.

Shankarji. "The Truth in Three Words." Review of *Be Here Now*, by Ram Dass. Amazon.com, Customer Review, July 11, 2000.

Bibliography

Vineyard USA. "Core Values and Beliefs." https://vineyardusa.org/about/core-values-beliefs/#.

Wallace, Daniel B. "The Witness of the Spirit in Romans 8:16: Interpretation and Implications." Who's Afraid of the Holy Spirit? An Investigation into the Ministry of the Spirit of God Today." *Bible.org*. December 14, 2005. https://bible.org/seriespage/2-witness-spirit-romans-816-interpretation-and-implications/.

www.ingramcontent.com/pod-product-compliance
Lightning Source LLC
Chambersburg PA
CBHW020849160426
43192CB00007B/852